Journeys
With Grief

A Collection of Articles about Love, Life, and Loss

HOSPICE FOUNDATION
OF AMERICA

Ordering information:
Hospice Foundation of America
1710 Rhode Island Avenue, NW #400
Washington, DC 20036
Toll-free: 800-854-3402
Web site: www.hospicefoundation.org

Amy S. Tucci, President/CEO

Editor: Kenneth J. Doka
Managing Editor: Lisa McGahey Veglahn
Layout and Design: Kristen Baker
Editorial Assistance: Lindsey Currin and Robb Sames

Publisher's Cataloging-in-Publication
(Provided by Quality Books, Inc.)

> Journeys with grief / Kenneth J. Doka, editor.
>   p. cm.
>   Includes index.
>   LCCN 2012947512
>   ISBN 978-1-893349-15-5
>
>   1. Grief. 2. Loss (Psychology) 3. Bereavement--
> Psychological aspects. 4. Death--Psychological aspects.
> I. Doka, Kenneth J.

BF575.G7J68 2012   155.9'37
                      QBI12-600208

ABOUT HOSPICE FOUNDATION OF AMERICA

Hospice Foundation of America (HFA) is a non-profit, charitable organization providing leadership in the development and application of hospice and its philosophy of care. Founded in 1983, HFA works to further discussion and awareness around death, grief, and care at the end of life through programs of professional development, public education and information, research, and support of hospice and bereavement programs. HFA offers extensive information about hospice care and grief and bereavement at hospicefoundation.org and provides a toll-free phone and email service to individuals and families seeking guidance about terminal illness, hospice care, palliative care, caregiving and grief.

ALSO AVAILABLE

Journeys: A Newletter to Help in Bereavement
Journeys Special Issues

Ordering information:

Call Hospice Foundation of America:
800-854-3402

Order online on HFA's Web site:
store.hospicefoundation.org

Or write:

Hospice Foundation of America
1710 Rhode Island Avenue, NW #400
Washington, DC 20036

COVER ART

Lights for the Darkness
Mary Jones, RN
Hands of Hope Hospice
St. Joseph, MO

The cover art was selected from hospices nationwide during HFA's *Journeys* artwork collection in spring, 2012.

Contents

Journeys
With Grief

A Collection of Articles about Love, Life, and Loss

HOSPICE FOUNDATION
OF AMERICA

Introduction

In 1994, Hospice Foundation of America (HFA) began publishing *Journeys: A Newsletter to Help in Bereavement.* We saw a need for a newsletter that would combine the most current information on grief, written by some of the best experts in the field, with the personal stories of individuals who had experienced loss. Our *Journeys* newsletter reaches tens of thousands of subscribers, through individual subscriptions and mailings from caring organizations such as hospices, hospitals, and funeral homes.

The Hospice Foundation of America is deeply committed to supporting people who are grieving, and *Journeys* is an integral part of that mission. Inherent in the name is that each of us has to find our own pathway as we experience grief. There are no universal stages, no definitive list of things we must do as we encounter grief, nor any set reaction we should or must have. Each of our journeys with loss is distinct—as individual as a fingerprint or snowflake. Yet the journey need not be lonely. This collection of articles is our way of making that journey with you.

HFA always keeps three goals in mind when selecting articles for *Journeys.* The first is to offer some guideposts—to validate the experience grievers might be having. A common question from those who are grieving is, "Am I normal?" As we journey with grief, we often travel without bearings. We may feel confused and distracted, and well-meaning friends and family might offer conflicting advice. One of the goals of *Journeys,* then, is simply reassurance. Our reactions, however different, are part of our personal experience with grief.

A second goal is to offer suggestions for coping. While grief is unique, we can learn from the experiences of others. These suggestions are presented as options that we have as we grieve. We might try those that seem helpful, ignoring others that do not seem to speak to us or to our ways of coping.

Finally, we like to think that each article in *Journeys* offers one final gift—*hope.* Though we journey with a significant loss throughout our lives, most of us do find that over time, the intensity of the reactions we are experiencing fades, and we are able to function as well as we did prior to the loss. Some of us may even grow as we grieve, developing fresh talents and abilities, learning new things about ourselves, and even deepening our spirituality.

Journeys with Grief allows us to place, in one book, the contributions of many authors, developed over decades of publication. We have included articles by experts in the field, touching on many of the most common concerns expressed by grievers. The "Because You Asked" sections answer real-life questions that have been submitted over the years. We also are pleased to include personal stories, written by those grieving a loss of someone close to them. These stories give a different and deeply meaningful perspective into this journey.

We can read *Journeys with Grief* in many ways. Some of us may choose to read it from beginning to end, gleaning whatever lessons make sense along the way. Others may decide to read the sections or articles that particularly speak to specific concerns. *Beginning the Journey* offers an overview of the grieving process. These initial pieces affirm the individuality of our grief, and remind us to shed any preconceptions we may have or that others offer as we begin our journey. The articles offer survival tips, reaffirming the support that can be available.

Grief is an unpredictable journey. *Journeys with Feelings* provides advice as we struggle to cope with the varied and complex emotions that we may experience with loss. We are also reminded that grief affects us in other ways—spiritually, behaviorally, physically, even in the ways we think.

Distinct losses and difficult problems can complicate our sense of loss. *Personal Journeys* touches on some of these circumstances and offers ways that others have coped.

Grief is an uneven journey. We can best think of the grieving process as a roller coaster, full of ups and downs, highs and lows. Like many roller coasters, the ride tends to be rougher in the beginning; the lows may be deeper and longer. The difficult periods should become less intense and shorter as time goes by; yet special times, like holidays or anniversaries, can still bring about a strong sense of grief. *Journeys through the Holidays* offers sage counsel as we approach these events, both familiar holidays and some that may be more "hidden," like Mother's or Father's Day.

Grief is a difficult journey as well. We need to be prepared. We should take good care of ourselves. Eating and sleeping well, and getting adequate exercise, are essential as we embark on this most difficult passage. *Challenges on the Journey* addresses some of these difficulties and offers some strategies in approaching them.

We need not travel alone. Others may share our grief—sometimes expressing it in helpful ways, other times perhaps making it more challenging. *Help for the Journey* reminds us of the ways that others may influence our grief, and how we might find additional support and guidance. Sharing our feelings with a close friend, in a journal, through a support group, or with a professional counselor, can be very helpful. A local hospice or funeral home can provide additional information about bereavement services in the community. We can find help for the journey from others and from the sources of strength within us.

Finally, grief is a continuing journey. We never lose the bond with people we love. They remain part of our lives. So it is not unusual that we may experience surges of grief even years after our loss. *Moving Forward on the Journey* reaffirms that these surges too are part of the experience. It may be that years later, perhaps when a child marries or a new grandchild is born, we find our joy intermixed with a sense of grief that someone we love is not here to share in the moment. That experience is normal; we always continue the connection to the ones we have loved. Yet by understanding that such surges are themselves part of the journey, that we always simultaneously deal with the challenge of coping with loss and the challenge of reconstructing a life now changed by loss, we can realistically hope that even in grief we can learn and grow. We can hope, even know, that we will survive.

Like grief, there is no right or wrong way to journey through this book. We simply hope it is a valued tool.

The journey with grief can be difficult and lonely. But we at the Hospice Foundation of America hope that *Journeys with Grief* can be like a candle. It may not make the journey easier or less lonely; but by illuminating the terrain, it can be more understandable and less frightening.

Beginning the Journey

We All Grieve

Whenever we face loss, we experience grief. Our reactions are unique and individual; none of us experience grief in the same way.

Not only are we different, but our losses are different. Some may grieve a spouse, others a child, parent, sibling, or friend. Each of these relationships is unique. Some may have been close; others may have had more tension or conflict. Circumstances may differ. Some losses are sudden, while others follow a prolonged illness. And we may each be able to draw upon different levels of support.

As we experience loss, we may need to remind ourselves of these basic facts. Sometimes we wonder why we do not respond as others, even our family members, do. But each of us is different.

Because each loss is unique, we may experience a wide range of emotions. We may feel anger—at God, towards the person who died, perhaps towards someone who we feel is not responding the way we'd like him or her to respond. We may feel guilt. Could we have done something differently? We may even feel responsible for the loss.

Other emotions are common. Feelings of sadness, longing for the person's presence, jealousy of others who have not experienced our loss, even relief that a prolonged illness has ended, may trouble us, but these are normal and natural responses to grief. Grief may affect us in other ways. For some, the experience of grief may be physical: aches and pains, difficulty eating or sleeping, fatigue. We may constantly think of the person, even replaying in our mind some final episode or experience. Grief can affect our spiritual selves, too. We may struggle to find meaning in our loss; our relationship with our faith beliefs may change.

I often describe grief as a roller coaster. It is full of ups and downs, highs and lows, times that we may think we are doing better and times that we are sure we are not. The metaphor reminds us that our sense of progress may feel very uneven.

But there are things we can do to help ourselves as we experience grief. First, it is important to accept the fact that we are grieving. Take time to grieve. Realize that life will be different, and sometimes difficult; we need to be gentle with ourselves.

Second, we can learn from the ways we have handled loss before. We need to draw on our resources—the coping skills we have, our own sources of support, and our spiritual strengths. And from earlier experiences, we can learn the mistakes we need to avoid.

We do not have to struggle alone. We can share our grief with family and friends. We can seek help from clergy or counselors. Librarians and bookstores can recommend books that can assist us as we grieve. Hospices and funeral homes may be able to suggest support groups and other community resources to help as we begin this difficult journey.

—KD

The Shock of Loss

Death is a harsh reality to grasp. The loss of a loved one can feel unreal, like a disturbing dream. We wish we could wake up and be free of this unwanted reality. We may know that a loved one is very ill or in the process of dying, yet the finality of death always feels sudden, shocking, and unbelievable.

When shocked, we walk through the first moments, hours, or even weeks afterward, like sleepwalkers. Experiences and conversations can be blurred or hazy. We may not yet feel any of the deep feelings of grief. People in shock can appear to be behaving normally without a lot of emotion because the news hasn't fully sunk in yet.

Numbness is our natural protection when facing any kind of trauma. Detached from the reality of our loss, we may be able to function pretty well at first. This can be confusing to us and to the people around us when we expect full-blown grief and suffering that we don't yet feel.

In the days or weeks to come, we usually break through this numbness to feel the full extent of our mixed and intense feelings— feelings like sadness, anger, longing, loneliness, guilt, resentment, and regret. Fully immersed in the grieving process, we then may feel flooded with our tears and emotions.

One difficult aspect of the grieving process is that we may feel shocked by our bad news many times in the days that follow the actual event. Because death is so hard to digest, it is as if we have to keep hearing it again and again in order to accept it.

We may keep ourselves awake at night obsessing about our loss or the impact it is having on us. We may fall asleep relatively easily, only to wake up in the middle of the night as if we just heard the bad news. And then we grieve anew. This process of rediscovering our loss makes most of us feel a little "crazy," yet this is how we process grief. We may be very uncomfortable but we are not crazy.

During the day, we may get involved in tasks or conversations and temporarily forget our loss until something reminds us. Then we are jolted again with a sense of disbelief and distress. Just being asked, "How are you?" can catapult us into remembering that something terrible has occurred. Even months later, the realization that someone we love is gone forever can come as an unwanted surprise.

It helps to recognize that shock is a natural part of grief that may occur many times before the actuality of our loss sinks in. Even though it makes us feel off-balance, it is part of how we process painful experiences, part of how we heal. In time, as we accept the truth of our loss, we will feel less and less shocked by it. But it is not unusual years later to have a moment of disbelief and again wonder how this could have happened. Death is hard to accept.

Most of all, we need to remember that even though the grieving process is uncomfortable and that loss itself is shocking, we can eventually acknowledge and accept our loss. We will remember our lost loved ones forever, but we do not need to grieve their absence forever.

—JT

In the Beginning: The Gift of Spiritual Coping Tools

The early days of the grieving process are always difficult. A wide variety of emotions overtakes our lives when the process of coping with loss begins. It can be surprising when the initial period of loss is so confusing and painful. In a spiritual sense, one can experience powerful adjustment periods that help the griever accept the fact of death. These adjustment periods become gifts when viewed as spiritual tools rather than pain to be avoided.

The gift of tears. Persons who are grieving often find crying disturbing. Many times, much effort goes into not showing the pain, as we judge crying to be a sign of weakness. "Adults don't cry in public!" "Big boys don't cry!" "She's holding up so well!" Our society devalues the gift of tears, but it might be helpful if we think of tears as merely another form of language. Tears are the language that we used upon entering this world; it is only the heartless individual who could ignore the cries of an infant or child. In our adult life we sometimes shed tears when what we have to say is beyond the scope of ordinary language. Tears can be a gift to us when we cannot adequately express what we feel in our hearts.

The gift of numbness. The initial days after a loss are filled with emotion and activity. Describing this time as a "flood of emotions" is probably an oversimplification. Feelings of loss, disbelief, anger, fear, guilt, loneliness, and anxiety are but a sampling of possible reactions. This combination of emotions is just too much to understand and assimilate. For most individuals, this period is like a spiritual tranquilizer when the reality of loss is just too great for the moment.

This early gift of numbness enables us to get through the initial days. As time begins to pass, these emotions will again appear when it is possible for us to deal with them.

The gift of companionship. One of the most important gifts bestowed upon those who grieve is the company of friends and family. There is normally a genuine outpouring of love and support toward those who lose a loved one. Visitations at the funeral home and the family residence following a notification of death frequently surprise the bereaved. Food and flowers are expressions of care and concern, attempting to meet basic needs for nurturing and support. It is important to recognize this important spiritual support.

Most faiths share the belief that the love of their God is seen through the love expressed by people on earth. If we ask, "Where is God when I am in so much pain?" the answer could be found in the visit, the phone call, the sympathy card, and yes, even the tenth meat tray or casserole. Grieving individuals need to remember the visits and the offers of help and utilize them to bring spiritual consolation and support. Just like tears and numbness, these spiritual gifts help us to cope in the early days of grief.

—MW

Love and Vulnerability

To love at all is to be vulnerable. Love anything, and your heart will certainly be wrung and probably be broken. If you want to make sure of keeping it intact, you must give your heart to no one, not even to an animal. Wrap it carefully round with hobbies and little luxuries; avoid all entanglements; lock it up safe in the casket or coffin of your selfishness. But in that casket—safe, dark, motionless, airless—it will change. It will not be broken; it will become unbreakable, impenetrable, irredeemable. . . .

This paragraph, from *The Four Loves* by C.S. Lewis (Mariner Books, 1971), offers both a keen diagnosis and two important cautions for bereaved persons. When we wonder why we are so devastated and heartbroken by the death of someone we loved—even an animal—Lewis' answer is that by giving our heart to that person we have made ourselves vulnerable. In loving another, we expose ourselves to the possibility of pain. Grief is simply the price we now must pay for having loved.

The cautions that follow from this for bereaved persons are of two types. The first caution reminds us that we need to appreciate our grief as the price we are now paying for having loved. Our grief is not wrong or unhealthy or abnormal or something we should just get over. On the contrary, our grief is something to be honored, just as we honored the love that enriched our life.

—CC

Because You Asked

Am I Normal?

*Since my husband's recent death, I've been doing strange things.
I cry for no reason as I wander aimlessly around the house. Sometimes I set an extra place for him at the table. When the telephone
rings, I think he is calling. I've become so absent-minded that I
renewed a subscription for his golf magazine and I don't even play
the game. I listen for his footsteps, especially in the evening, when
he would normally return from work. My thinking and judgment
seem so impaired that I feel like I am falling apart. Am I going
crazy?*

These symptoms are not a sign of mental illness and
you are not alone; many grieving people have similar
experiences. When asked to comment on her adjustment
to widowhood, the late-distinguished actress Helen Hayes
remarked, "I was just as crazy as you can be and still be at
large."

It is natural to be overwhelmed when your husband has
just died. Your mind is preoccupied with your devastating loss. Confusion, aimlessness, and constant weeping are
all indicators of your pain and despair. When absence becomes the greatest presence, you have transformed the past
into the present. By wishing and daydreaming, you have
attempted to bring your loved one magically back to life.

Your brain has not been damaged. You are emotionally
and physically depleted. Death has wounded you. There is

probably no crisis more stressful than the loss of someone you loved.

Forgive yourself when you are not as reliable and responsible as you once were. Give yourself permission to be inconsistent and unpredictable without punishing and criticizing yourself. Develop an acceptance of the brief periods of irrational feelings and chaotic bewilderment.

If it would ease your mind, you might consult a grief counselor or seek help from a support group. In most cases, these strange actions and thoughts are temporary. They gradually fade and disappear as you continue your journey through the mourning process.

Incidentally, Helen Hayes, who was "as crazy as can be and still be at large," later returned to acting, and she brought new life into the theater for decades.

—*EG*

How am I Expected to Grieve?

Grief is not predictable. We cannot time and plot our reactions. This type of approach makes us think that losses vary only insofar as different deaths may make us spend more or less time at a certain "stage." Such a theory belies our own individuality and the uniqueness of each particular loss.

Each of us has our own way we experience grief. For some of us, we may see grief as something we should deal with quickly—resuming our life as soon as we return to work, seemingly over our loss. Others are surprised by how long our grief lingers and how painful the process can be.

Grief is full of different tasks and processes. We not only have to cope with feelings but also accept the reality of the loss, redefine our beliefs now in the face of that loss, readjust to the daily realities of that loss, and decide the ways we will remember the person who died.

Grief is more than simply a set of feelings. In a significant loss, every aspect of our life is now changed.

We need to remember that grief is an uncertain and individual journey. However, a more realistic road map may make the journey with grief a little less frightening.

—KD

How Long Does Grief Last?

At one point or another, everyone who has ever grieved has wondered, "How long will this grief persist? How long must I feel sorrow and pain?" We don't like feeling uncomfortable. We detest that complex mix of feelings that grief brings. We may feel like victims of our feelings, wishing they would just disappear.

As a culture, we want everything to be quick and easy. We don't savor feelings any more than we savor the wide range of our varied life experiences. Like everything else that we hurry through in life, we may be obsessed with getting through our pain as quickly as possible, foregoing the difficult part of grief and sailing on right to recovery.

How long does grief take? The real answer is grief takes as long as it takes—a week, a month, a year, or even longer, depending on whom we have lost and how their death is affecting us. Grief is a process we must move through, not over or around. Even when we can temporarily ignore or deny our pain, it still exists. It will eventually erupt in some way, maybe at an inappropriate moment or during another illness. It is always better to admit our strong feelings, feel them, and then move through them so that we may move beyond them.

How do we move beyond the pain? What does it mean to move beyond? It means not being forever in pain over our loss. It doesn't mean we forget or stop loving the person we lost. We do not always have to grieve; we can remember without pain.

Too often, we hear the awful message that we never stop grieving, we never get over our loss. When we have no tools for overcoming sorrow, and when the world tries to shut us up, grief does go on longer than it should. But our attitude and outlook are important; the belief that we will never recover from a loss can become a self-fulfilling prophecy if we let it. When we believe we can recover, we do. It is important to trust that grief is not forever.

I believed I would grieve forever when my brother died. I kept sorrow alive for 14 years by the simple act of believing it was endless. I didn't know how to stop my grief. Grief that persists for years can hold us back—keep us living in the past, or keep us from loving the people who are still alive. I was stunted by my grief, afraid to trust, afraid to commit, and afraid to have children I might lose. It wasn't until a good therapist helped me express fully how much this loss hurt me that I was able to stop grieving.

No matter how much we may hurt today, we must remember that grief is temporary. Mourning does not have to last forever. We can finish crying and express all our many feelings around this loss.

We can find in ourselves the courage to recover and heal. We can begin to live fully and love again.

—JT

Survival Tips for Grief

So often after the loss of a loved one, we wonder how we can ever go on. Whenever we have to face a major loss, the grief journey may seem like a mountain that is too difficult to climb. It's important to know there are some steps you can take that will help ease that journey.

Allow your grief. No step is more important than this. Appreciate, accept, and allow your grief as a natural response to your loss. Let yourself feel your pain. Suppressed grief doesn't go away. Grief is a mix of many uncomfortable feelings. You may feel sad, angry, or filled with remorse, regret, or longing. All these feelings are natural.

Express your grief. Empty out your feelings. Cry when you need to cry. Be angry when you feel angry. Don't pretend to be stoic. The more you express your pain, the more you free yourself from it.

Be patient with yourself. Grief is a process that takes time. Healing from grief is not necessarily quick and easy, but it is possible. Trust that you can and will heal from your loss. The day will come when you can remember your loved one without pain.

Keep busy. You cannot dwell on your sorrow or your loss every waking moment. In the first flush of grief, you may feel you cannot control the extent of your suffering. But with friends and activities, you can form a plan that can be a lifeline.

Keep a journal. This can be a powerful method for expressing pain, as well as a means for having private, intimate time with yourself. Some feelings may be too hard to speak aloud, like anger or regret. Journal writing can serve as a release as well as a meaningful expression of yourself, which can speed up the process of your healing.

Exercise daily. Move your body. Walking, dancing, swimming, or whatever activity pleases you can help you feel better. Through exercise, you build your physical strength, release tension, and keep yourself well. Exercise releases endorphins that will lift your mood.

Be willing to change things. It is natural to wish to keep things the way they were when our loved one was with us. Still, that doesn't keep them alive. My friend Ann kept her bedroom exactly as it was before her husband died 15 years ago. She might never have noticed until a visitor commented that the art on the wall was so masculine. Ann suddenly realized she was sleeping in her husband's room. We asked her, "What if it was your bedroom?" The next time I saw that room, it was transformed with color, frills, and flowers.

Although loss is never easy to face, we need to remember we can go on with our lives, taking care of ourselves in the process.

—JT

Journeys with Feelings

The Feelings of Grief

One of the things we need to do as we grieve is to acknowledge and accept the range of emotions we experience. Our feelings are what they are. We cannot control our feelings; we can only validate them, recognizing that they are part of our journey with grief.

Some of these reactions—such as sadness, loneliness, and yearning—are readily recognizable as manifestations of grief. How could we not be sad, not miss someone who we so loved, who was part of our life?

We may be anxious or fearful as we now face life without a person whom we counted on for advice and support. In other cases the very circumstances of the death may make us realize how fragile life can be.

Other emotions may trouble us. We may struggle with guilt, which can come from many sources. We may feel bad over the things we said or left unsaid. We may feel guilty that we are alive when that person is now dead. We may even feel guilty about our grief, worrying if we are doing too well or not well enough. Our feelings of grief do not always have to be rational to be real. We may experience a sense of relief that the person's suffering is over and perhaps that our suffering as we watched that person die is now over as well. This sense of relief is both natural and understandable. Yet for some of us, this sense of relief can also prompt guilt.

Anger may be another troubling emotion. We may find that we lash out at others or we may even be angry at the person who died. Anger is very natural in grief; acknowledging that we are angry can help us deal with that strong emotion without it becoming destructive.

Some emotions may be positive. We may have a deep sense of thankfulness that we shared our life together. We may feel proud that we held up so well or took such good care of the person as he or she was dying. These emotions, too, are part of grief.

Not everyone experiences such strong emotions. Some of us feel in vivid colors, others in pastels. This is part of the individuality of grief.

Once we understand our feelings, we can further explore them. What is prompting these emotions? Are there times that I am more likely to experience certain feelings? What are the roots of my guilt or my anger? How are these emotions affecting me or others? Once we understand our emotions, we can find ways to deal with our feelings. For example, Elaine found that being alone on Sundays, a day that she and her husband spent together, triggered feelings of loneliness. Now aware of that pattern, she now plans to spend Sundays with family and friends.

Sometimes we can deal with our emotions on our own—perhaps by journaling or keeping a diary of our reactions. Other times we may find it helpful to address these issues with others—a close friend, counselor, clergyperson, or support group. It matters less how we find it useful to address our grief; it simply matters that we do.

—*KD*

Depression and Grief

My wife had been sick for several years; for four months before she died she was being cared for by home hospice, but I was always the main person caring for her. Now that I'm alone, my children want me to come visit but I don't have the energy or the desire. I feel so hopeless and sad, like I'm out of control. Please help.

Sometimes, when we're a caregiver, we don't realize the toll that it takes on us. Although we may acknowledge our physical exhaustion, we don't expect the emotional exhaustion that follows the death. Our energy level is down and we often feel depleted.

However, while grief is painful, most responses are a result of the sadness associated with the death of a loved one. There are things you can do to help you feel more in control.

Recognize that you need to care for yourself. This is not easy, especially when you've always cared for others.

Keep up with your physical exams. When we're caring for others, we frequently neglect or don't have the time to care for ourselves.

Get some physical activity. Even walking around the block can be refreshing.

Be sure to eat regularly. Even if you don't want to cook for yourself, many supermarkets sell takeout meals.

Establish a new sleep regime. It may be soothing to sleep with a light on or while listening to music.

Return to activities that you've enjoyed in the past. Become involved in groups at your church or synagogue, or other committees and clubs.

Seek help. This may be hard if you've always been independent and have never asked for help in the past.

A bereavement support group might help validate your feelings. Being with others who have had a similar loss can be helpful in ways you have never imagined.

Although feeling down is an expected response after a loved one dies, we each grieve in different ways and there is no timeframe for when grief ends. If some of the steps above don't seem to help, or you continue to feel even more helpless, it may be time to talk with your physician. Be sure to let him or her know about your loss, in order to help make a medical determination between sadness and clinical depression.

If your sadness is more than grief and is actually clinical depression, there are medications and therapies that can be helpful. Your physician will discuss these with you.

—*SS*

Emotional Contradictions: Grief and Relief

"**W**as I wrong to wish for George to die?" Betty asked her minister. "It hurt so badly to give him up, but it was so hard to see him get weaker and weaker. I couldn't wish for that to go on and on. I prayed that he could be at rest."

George had been seriously ill for more than two years. After months of being confined to a wheelchair, he became bedridden. He became more and more confused before his death.

Betty was torn by her conflicting emotions. She grieved for George, feeling a vast emptiness in her life, missing the companionship of a long marriage. She was also grateful that George no longer had to endure days of just staring blankly at the ceiling. She was relieved not to have to be changing bed linens every few hours and doing load after load of laundry.

It crossed her mind again and again that it was somehow not right to feel relieved. Was it self-centered to want to be free of the heavy responsibilities that had worn her down during the years? After all, she had married George "for better or for worse."

The psychological name for such conflicting emotions is ambivalence. We are not strangers to divided feelings. We have a hard time making decisions because we want to go somewhere and at the same time don't want to go. We may simultaneously love someone dearly and be very annoyed with her or him. We may feel profound grief when someone dies, while also being glad the suffering is over.

We struggle with divided feelings. Sometimes it is just confusing. We struggle to understand how we can feel joy and sadness, loss and gain. Often it is more than simple confusion. We think or feel that one side of our divided feelings is good and the other side is less worthy. It is all right to grieve for someone we loved, but we have some questions about feeling relieved, even glad, that the end has come.

This is particularly true when we recognize that we have not only lost, but also gained. We feel somewhat selfish by seeing that we have benefited from the death. We may have been relieved of the heavy burdens of care; we may have inherited from the estate of the deceased.

Betty found it less difficult to express her grief than to share her relief that George's increasingly limited life had ended and that the heavy burden of caring for him was over. She was reluctant to tell anyone that she had wished for George's death.

When she finally found courage to share her mixed feelings with her minister, his understanding helped her to accept these contradictory feelings. Her pastor pointed out that both her deep sense of loss and her grateful feeling that George's struggle was over had valid explanations and required no further justification. She was free to accept her divided feelings.

Counselors use the term "ventilating feelings." Bringing them to the open air, talking about them, or sharing them with a trusted loved one or counselor can bring a release from the struggle to understand and accept our mixed emotions.

—PI

Anger is a Natural Part of Grief

After my brother David died in a car accident, I never allowed myself to admit that I was angry at him for leaving me. Had I felt free to tell the truth, I would have said I was furious. But I didn't admit my anger for many years.

Many who grieve say, "How can I be angry at my beloved for dying?" We know they couldn't help dying. We feel aghast or ashamed at the idea of blaming them, so we stuff down and deny our feelings. Nonetheless these feelings exist within us, whether we find them acceptable or not.

Many people do in fact feel angry when someone we love dies. We feel angry at being abandoned, angry at the extent of our pain, angry that our life is changed, angry that managing our grief feels difficult, and angry that the world suddenly feels different—empty, unsafe, or lonely.

When we doubt the legitimacy or the naturalness of our feelings around a loss, we shut ourselves off from our own depths and deny our own experience.

But just because we deny feelings doesn't mean they don't exist. Swallowed feelings don't disappear. Instead, they may become the basis for unresolved grief, depression, anxiety, and even chronic physical symptoms. Allowing our feelings, whatever they may be, is essential to healing from grief.

As a culture, we are not comfortable with anger. Yet the feeling of anger itself is natural and not destructive; it's a feeling like any other. Still, most of us have not learned to accept anger as a natural part of human experience. We do get angry, and still we are good people. This is just one of many varied and intense emotions in response to losing someone we love.

Intense feelings need to be expressed, not denied. Being able to say out loud, "I am angry," may be all that it takes to dissipate this intense emotion. Then again, we may need to say, "I am angry" and express aloud all the stories and feelings that follow before the feelings resolve or disappear. To fully release anger, we may need to have some safe physical way to express it, like pounding a pillow, chopping wood, or yelling loudly in the privacy of our bathroom or out in the woods somewhere.

Anger can make us feel powerful in the face of experiences like loss, where we naturally feel pretty powerless. We may prefer to be angry so as not to appear vulnerable, openly tearful, or sad.

We can help someone else who is grieving by listening. We can say, "Tell me about your anger," instead of running away from such emotions. We may feel more comfortable hearing anecdotes about the dead person than the intense emotions around loss. However, listening to another's pain without offering judgments or advice is a rare gift to give.

Remember, anger is a natural part of grief. Suppressing or swallowing feelings delays our healing. Voicing our feelings, expressing anger and any other emotions, empowers us, strengthens us, and helps us heal.

—JT

The Loneliness of Grief

Loneliness is a natural part of grief. And it is one of the more trying aspects of accepting a loss. When a loved one dies, there is a hole in our lives that no one and nothing else can fill. It is as if no one else can know or understand our loss. Our intense and mixed feelings of grief separate us from other people. It is that uncomfortable feeling of being lonely in a crowd, of being in the middle of a party or on a busy street, but feeling invisible, unknown in the midst of your pain.

Anyone who has lost a loved one knows that familiar ache of missing those who are gone, the loneliness and longing for their presence, their companionship, their voice, their smell, and who they were in our lives.

We also have to face the sense of loneliness that comes from being in the world bereft. While we who are grieving may feel everything is out of sync, in contrast, the rest of the world looks orderly. People seem to be going along in their everyday easy way, as if nothing is wrong. To those of us who have lost someone dear, everything is wrong. The dissimilarity between us and those around us makes us feel all the more lonely.

Another trying aspect of loneliness, which is more difficult to talk about, is that we may feel a sense of having been abandoned by the one who died, regardless of the actual circumstances. Our imaginations play with the idea that "If he really loved me, he would not have died." We may feel as if we have been left, deserted and alone, even if it isn't true. We ask ourselves privately, "How could he do this to me?"

Feelings of abandonment are among the most agonizing feelings that we must endure and conquer. The secret here is to remember the reality that death is something we cannot control. Our loved ones didn't die to hurt us; they didn't mean for us to feel abandoned.

We must remember too that we do not have to feel like victims of our loneliness. Sometimes a change of perspective helps. People who have lost long-term partners have found a variety of ways to deal with the gap in their lives. A widow I know couldn't bear staring at her husband's empty seat at the dinner table, so she sat there herself; it changed her perspective.

We can break through our loneliness by making one telephone call, speaking one word to another person. We can share our feelings with someone we trust, let someone else into our private world. The people around us—family, friends, colleagues, caring professionals—are all part of our support system, if we let them. Including other people in our lives helps us. We don't have to face the isolating feelings and the loneliness of grief all alone.

—JT

The Strangeness of Grief

A while ago, someone asked me what was the most common way that bereaved individuals described their experience of grief. I thought for a few moments. It was not, as I reflected, the words one would generally expect—*sad, lonely,* or *unhappy.* The word that so many people use to describe their experience of grief was *strange.* It makes sense. So much of the experience of grief is so odd.

We may experience all sorts of reactions—strong intense emotions that seem to wash over us in waves. There may be times that, at the least provocation, we cry. Other times, we may wonder why we are not weeping. We may feel that everything is surreal—that we are going through the motions but are strangely unconnected to anything or anyone around us. We may struggle to find some meaning and purpose in our life. It may be difficult to concentrate or focus. Even physically we may feel different—somehow aware of every ache and pain.

We may even have strange experiences. There may be moments we feel the presence of the person who died. We may dream of the person or hear a voice or sound that reminds us of that individual.

We may find that others treat us strangely. They may seem uncomfortable as they approach us, not knowing what to say. They may feel awkward around us, wondering if we will burst into tears.

Our world now seems so different. The things we once took for granted such as eating, watching television, going out, or even sleeping, now seem so far removed from how they once were. It is like we have to learn everything, every experience, anew.

Margaret Stroebe and Hans Schut, two researchers from the Netherlands, describe grief as a "dual process"—mourning a loss even as we adjust to a new life. I see that duality so frequently in my grief groups as people experience these twin mandates of grief. For example, the widow who at one moment describes her loneliness at the loss of her spouse, who always drove—even as she celebrates the triumph of her first driver's license. When we grieve we bounce back and forth between these dual demands. That, too, seems strange.

Grief is a strange experience. That is why validation is so important. As we share our grief with others—friends, family members, counselors, or in support groups—we realize that we are not alone in our experiences. That knowledge may not make the experience less strange, but we do know that it is normal to feel strange. To live life without someone we love—someone who was an important part of our life—is strange.

—*KD*

Better Than I Should Be?

We always begin our support group asking if anyone has anything they wish to discuss. One woman raised her hand. "I think," Sylvia stated tentatively, "that I am doing better than I should be doing." She seemed worried that there was something she was missing, and that soon the pain of grief would come crashing down upon her.

The truth is that her response was as natural and as normal as others in the group. A recent study showed that just less than half of people surveyed showed relatively few manifestations of grief and an ability to function well even after a loss. The researchers labeled these grievers "resilient."

These people shared certain characteristics. For example, resilient grievers reported fewer losses—that is, one loss did not follow close behind another. The deaths they experienced were generally not sudden. Most said that they found great comfort in having had the opportunity to say "goodbye" to the person who died. In many cases, the deaths were not perceived to be "preventable." Resilient grievers often saw little they could have done to prevent the loss. Of course, some of these factors are hard to control as they relate to past history or the conditions surrounding the death.

Grievers in the study who fell into the "resilient" category also reported experiencing fewer psychological problems or stressors prior to the loss, and most noted that they had good social support. Many expressed a strong sense of spirituality that offered comfort and guidance.

Resilient grievers tend to have an optimistic mindset. Part of this mindset is a belief that even the most tragic situations offer opportunities for learning and personal growth. Sylvia strongly believed this. The loss of her spouse was an exceedingly painful event. Yet, rather than being overwhelmed by the changes she experienced in her life, Sylvia looked at them as a challenge. Each new accomplishment—even mundane ones, such as doing the household bills—was viewed as a personal triumph.

Resilient grievers may share a belief that something good can come from even the worst events. Alan's son died in a terribly tragic accident; on a hike, his son slipped and tumbled off a cliff. While Alan continues to grieve deeply for his son, he takes comfort in the fact that a new guardrail that he helped install will keep other adolescents from a similar fate.

Resilient grievers in the study noted that they consciously tried to think of positive memories of the person who died; over time, they reported these comforting memories would spontaneously emerge. Sylvia, for example, would return to a beach her husband loved. "I would replay events in my mind—very consciously at first. Then, soon, whenever I was at a beach, even if I saw a photo of a beach, I would be flooded by these warm thoughts."

We need not worry then if we are doing better than we think we should be doing; we can be comforted by it. And even resilient grievers will have times when grief does come to the forefront. For those who are not there yet, perhaps the lessons we can learn from those who are doing "better than we should" can offer some help, even in the midst of our own grief.

—KD

Personal Journeys

The Loss of a Child

You never expect to bury your children, no matter how old or young. The death of a child is a deeply troubling loss that challenges parents on many levels.

You will probably experience a range of emotions. The inherent unfairness of such a loss may cause tremendous anger; such anger is natural. However, it may drive away the very people you need for support at this difficult time.

Guilt also may be intense. You may grapple with the notion, however unrealistic, that you could have prevented the death. You may succumb to the irrational belief that parents can always protect their children. You may feel guilty about things that were said or left unsaid, reviewing those normal moments of parent-child relationships. You may fear that this is a punishment for some imagined sin of your own past or feel guilty that you live and your child does not. You may even feel guilty about your grief, wondering if it is too intense or not strong enough. You may experience other emotions as well—loneliness, yearning, anxiety, or helplessness.

Grief is not just emotions. You may feel unwell physically. It may be difficult to concentrate or focus; images of your child may flood you at times. You may behave differently—perhaps withdrawing, or becoming lethargic, apathetic, or aggressive. You might find yourself in constant activity as you try to fill the empty spaces and avoid your pain.

The death of a child is traumatic and shatters assumptions about how the world should be. It may raise doubt about your beliefs as you ask questions that cannot be answered.

A child's death is a family loss. Everyone in the family is affected—fathers, mothers, brothers and sisters, grandparents, aunts and uncles. This may make it more difficult to get support from those around you as each person copes with his or her deeply personal sense of loss.

This reality can be true even between the parents of the child who has died. Grief is very individual; you may each find that your experience with grief, the way you express it, and how you deal with it, is different. This does not mean that one person loved the child more. Rita wondered about that. When her daughter died of sudden infant death syndrome (SIDS), she was constantly crying. Her husband was more active—supporting the SIDS Foundation and talking with other parents who had experienced this type of loss. They both deeply loved their child, yet they grieved each in their own way.

This loss may affect every aspect of your relationship. Some couples wrestle with intimacy, needing the physical closeness even as they may feel reluctant to re-engage sexually. While the death of a child may strain relationships, there is no evidence to support the myth that the strain is permanent.

Since grief presents such special challenges when a child dies, it is important not to grieve alone. Support groups such as The Compassionate Friends, one-on-one counseling, or reading books about loss can offer support, validation, and hope that you can survive this most difficult journey with grief, and deserve to be supported on that journey.

—KD

When the Griever is Intellectually Disabled

There is an old Buddhist proverb that reminds us that we are all like all others, some others, and no other. I think of that proverb when I work with persons with intellectual disabilities.

Like all of us, persons with intellectual disabilities experience loss and grief. Like all of us, this grief is expressed in many ways—physically, emotionally, cognitively, spiritually, and behaviorally. Crying, silence and withdrawal, sleep disturbances, physical complaints, and resistance to change are not uncommon experiences.

Yet there are difficulties in processing grief that may be shared by others with similar conditions. Depending on the level of disability, persons with intellectual disabilities may have a difficult time understanding death. Hence they may struggle with the notion that death is permanent—constantly asking when the person who died will return or when they can speak with that individual. Their emotional expression may be distorted.

Years ago, I counseled a young woman with intellectual disabilities whose mother had just died. Whenever this woman was agitated or nervous she would giggle. She told me the story of her mother's death with this nervous titter. Other persons with intellectual disabilities may have a "positive bias," a sunny disposition that masks their deep sense of loss. Others may have severe conceptual or speech limitations that make it difficult to understand their needs.

Yet whether or not someone can be understood is a poor measure of whether they can understand. All but perhaps the most severely disabled feel and understand the loss of someone they know and love.

We can help by validating that loss. One of the dangers is that the grief of individuals with intellectual disabilities will be ignored, or disenfranchised, by others. Sometimes it is the result of over protectiveness that makes us pretend that such individuals are spared the pain of grief. In other cases we may be fearful of our own abilities; we wish to avoid coping with a grief and pain that is difficult for even us to understand.

People with intellectual disabilities have the same needs as all of us in grief. They need to be supported by others. They need to have their concerns addressed and their questions patiently answered.

They need to have the opportunities to participate in funeral rituals in a way that is comfortable. This may mean that a private time be set aside so that they can attend a special viewing with their closest family and friends. It may mean that they attend the funeral rituals with the special support of someone they trust. Like all of us, persons with intellectual disabilities need choices—and the respect those choices denote.

As with all of us, persons with intellectual disabilities grieve like none of us. All grief is ultimately individual and unique. Our grief is a combination of the highly individual relationship we shared with the person who died as well as the distinctive ways that we each cope with loss. We all, whatever our level of intellectual abilities and functioning, form attachments and experience loss.

—KD

Grieving a Soldier

Bonnie Carroll is the President and Founder of the Tragedy Assistance Program for Survivors (TAPS), the national Veterans Service Organization providing peer based emotional support, grief and trauma resources and information, casualty casework assistance and crisis intervention for all those affected by the death of a loved one serving in, or in support of, the armed forces. Ms. Carroll founded TAPS following the death of her husband, Brigadier General Tom Carroll, in an Army C-12 plane crash.

*T*here are things I will never forget. The knock on the front door that November morning, the solemn look in the eye of the Army officer who came to deliver the news, the morning paper that bore the headlines, "Soldiers killed...", and the feel of the heavy cloth of the folded flag that was gently placed in my arms at the graveside. I shall never forget the mournful notes of the bugle drifting out over the rows of silent headstones as the final honors were rendered at the cemetery. Those memories are with me forever.

For so long, those recollections were full of pain and sadness. They were sharp reminders of the day my world changed forever and they triggered a flood of tears. As time went on, there was a subtle shift. Did you know that the words to the famous musical piece "Taps" are actually a prayer? "Day is done, gone the sun, from the hills, from the lake, from the sky. All is well, safely rest, God is nigh." I once heard this sung and felt so healed and moved by these words.

As time passed, there would be other such shifts. Lee Vincent, the father of a Marine who died in an air crash, reminded us in an article in the TAPS newsletter that, "Every one of those we love had already risen far above the rest of our society in character, courage, honor and ability. And not an atom of that achievement can ever be lost or taken back. If they had lived, they would be proud today of who they are and what they are doing. Now, it's our duty to be proud for them."

So, it isn't about their death, it was about their life. The theme of the TAPS Survivor Seminar, held each Memorial Day weekend in Washington, DC, is "Remember the Love, Celebrate the Life, Share the Journey." We truly do honor those we love by cherishing the extraordinary lives others lived, regardless of the circumstances or geography of their death.

A TAPS mom shared these words of Ralph Waldo Emerson: "It is not length of life, but depth of life." The decision to join the military and protect and defend freedom, even if it means going into harm's way, is a courageous one, and it speaks to the character of the individual. Their life had depth, and even if cut short, was lived fully and richly.

I have learned many things in the years since Tom's death, and like to think of these as lessons he continues to teach me. Life is rarely understandable and often unfair. We are all living on borrowed time. Our loved one surely knew that time was precious and didn't waste a moment of it. They lived a life that may have been outwardly simple but was inwardly rich, and they showed how one person could inspire in others a powerful faith.

One of my husband's friends called him "incredibly, irrepressibly full of life" and asked "If he is not immortal, what of the rest of us?" Well, our loved ones are immortal. They will live forever in the memories—and hopefully, the deeds—of every life they have touched. Remember the joy it was to know them, to witness the things they said, the smiles they shared, the kindnesses they did, and how they laughed. That's how we all should remember them. And carry on in our hearts the great legacy they have given us.

From Wife to Widow

Several years ago, while visiting a resort with my husband, we heard laughter as we approached the dining room. A bus had pulled up in front of the lodge and scores of older women spilled out. Patiently anticipating each other's deliberate strides marked by age, the women linked arms as they entered. I wondered, were these women alone? Did they have surviving friends and family? Was this their new family? This image remained in my mind long after. But one thing was certain; their presence added a sparkle and a feeling of celebration to the mood that night.

Years later, when I became widowed, I recalled that evening and I felt a renewed sense of compassion and admiration for those women entering the dining hall. For the first time in my adult life, I was half of a couple. I knew that regardless of how long I lived, my husband would not be with me for celebrations, challenges, or when I die. I sorely missed telling him about my day and sharing all the little private jokes that each couple has between them. All of this was a stark reminder of my new status as a single, older, aging woman.

Regardless of how independent we are, there is something frightening about losing a significant other and our "other half." It felt as though a part of my identity had suddenly vanished with this loss, an identity that was so closely tied to another human being. I felt as though he took part of me with him; I still felt married and like somebody's wife.

One might ask, where in my heart can I keep my former life without becoming stuck in time? Will I ever love again? Some of these questions made me feel like I was 18 years old again, back to square one trying to determine who I am in my sixth decade of life. It somehow felt even more frightening than it did when I was younger because the death of a loved one forces us to face our own mortality.

Several years ago, while visiting friends in the Bahamas, I saw a banyan tree for the first time. I was mesmerized by the fact that as the tree grows, new roots descend from its branches, pushing into the ground and forming new trunks.

Like the banyan tree, we must expand and grow while keeping our support systems securely rooted. And like the seniors who stepped off that bus that evening, we must continue to find a song we want to sing in this dance we call life.

—MGW

When a Partner Dies

We share many intimate relationships. Marriage is, of course, the most common; yet there are others. We may live with another person. We may have a long dating relationship that has not led to either living together or marriage. Some may be with members of the other gender while others may be with same-sex partners.

In the end, though, only two things really matter. We loved that person. Now that partner has died, and grief has begun.

Grief is not isolated to marriage or familial relationships.

Each of us experiences grief in our own way. For some of us, the experience can be very physical—our bodies literally hurt. For others of us, grief may be more of an emotional experience—a roller coaster of feelings. In still other cases, grief may affect us spiritually or influence the ways we act. Grief may even have an effect on us cognitively, making it hard to focus or concentrate. Each of us will have our own unique combination of reactions as we experience loss and grief.

But while the grief reactions are similar to married couples, we may not have the same support that a married person does. We might have experienced this already. We may have found we had to explain our presence at the hospital or funeral home. We may have had to take vacation days to attend doctor's appointments or be by the bedside, as unmarried relationships are not acknowledged by our workplaces. We may find that the sympathy cards are few and far between. The grief is disenfranchised—unacknowledged by others.

It may even be that the funeral ritual was itself unsatisfying, because the relationship was overlooked or ignored. In such a case, we may need to create our own ritual privately, or possibly with a few trusted friends, to mourn the person we knew and the relationship we lost.

Others may simply not recognize the enormity of our loss or the intensity of our grief. While our grief may not have the same social support, we still must mourn when a partner dies. We need to find safe places to explore our feelings and reactions. This may be with an understanding close friend, a receptive support group, or a grief counselor.

The important thing is that we do not disenfranchise ourselves. We need to acknowledge our own grief and create our own opportunities to mourn. And we need to find others who can support us in our grief.

I facilitate a support group for men, who once reinforced these lessons. Most are older men who were widowed. Last year, a gay man who had lost his partner asked to join the group. He wondered how accepting the group would be; I wondered too, but encouraged him to attend.

He did, and tentatively told his story. At first the men were surprised, but clearly recognized the nature of his loss. There was a moment of awkward silence. Then one of the older men, a tough, retired steamfitter, put his hand on the younger man's shoulder. "But you loved him", the steamfitter asked gruffly but with compassion, "right?" The younger man tearfully nodded. "Then you belong here!" the older man assured him.

He was right. Grief, in the final analysis, is a measure of love.

—KD

Silent Loss: Mourning a Miscarriage

I never mourned my miscarriage; it happened so long ago. But recently, I met an old friend who had a child the age mine would have been. I kept thinking: "What would my daughter have been like?" Will I ever get over this?

M iscarriages occur in at least 20 percent of pregnancies, many in the first 12 weeks. While the physical needs of many women who miscarry are addressed, emotional needs may be neglected. But it is never too late to address unresolved hurt.

How do you mourn an unborn child? And how do you cope when well-meaning friends and family attempt to offer support and solace, but inflict greater pain instead?

Someone says, "You can have another baby," and you think, "But we are grieving this baby."

Someone says, "Be thankful you have other children," and you think, "But we wanted this baby, too."

Because of the lack of understanding, miscarriage has been called "the silent loss," often unrecognized by others, sometimes even by ourselves. It is important to acknowledge such a loss. You are still searching for the source of this heartbreak. Since you might have felt totally responsible for the baby's health, you might blame yourself for the miscarriage. Yet there is little medical evidence that a woman's activity will increase the likelihood of miscarriage; there isn't always any discernible cause.

But how can you grieve for your lost hopes and dreams? How can you mourn—not alone in silence —but with those whom you love?

Gather with family members or friends. This may provide both you and others an opportunity to share emotions that they have bottled up in an attempt to shield you from more pain.

Join a self-help group. Talking with other parents who have endured this similar anguish can be very beneficial.

Work with a therapist. A professional counselor can help you explore your unsettled expressions of bereavement.

Find healing in writing a letter or a poem. Light a candle on the date of the miscarriage or give a donation to a hospice or charity in loving memory.

Miscarriage leaves many unanswered questions, and the pain may at times seem vast and unending. Both for you and for those who suffer various types of "silent losses," heed the words of philosopher Cornel West: "To live is to wrestle with despair; yet never allow despair to have the last word."

—EG

When an Adult Child Dies

"If he were 12, everyone would understand my grief. Why can't they understand it now? Even though he was 42 years old, he was still my son."

Other parents who have experienced the death of an adult child often echo Sonya's comment. They may feel a lack of support, in part because it is focused on other survivors, such as the child's spouse or children, and in part because there simply is little recognition of the powerful bond that exists between parent and child once that child is independent. Whatever the reasons, the result is the same: the grief of the parent can be disenfranchised—meaning that grief is not fully recognized or supported by others.

The death of a child is an "out-of-order" death. As we do not expect our child to die before we do, we may feel a sense of injustice that challenges our spiritual beliefs.

These factors complicate an already difficult situation. This loss may be one of many that the parent is experiencing. As individuals age, they may have to relinquish cherished roles or activities. In short, this death may add to a litany of losses, complicating coping.

When adult children die, parents may lose a critical source of support in their own lives. The child may have provided emotional, physical, or even financial support. The parent may have experienced a sense of vicarious achievement in the child's successes. The parent may feel a deep sense of disappointment that the adult child never accomplished important goals. Sometimes the death of an adult child can affect other relationships; relations with the surviving spouse or grandchildren may change. Even family events may seem different now.

Parents may feel a lack of control that complicates the loss. They may have had little or no control over their child's medical treatment or even the funeral or burial.

How, then, can parents cope with such a loss? How can others offer support? First, it is critical to validate that grief, to recognize that the death of a child, regardless of age or circumstance, is always a horrendous event. Support is critical. If the parent is feeling as though he or she had little control over the funeral rituals or if these rituals were not meaningful, the parent may wish to gather his or her own friends for a ritual. Sonya did that; her friends, all of whom had been part of her son's life as well as Sonya's, could not join her at his funeral 2,000 miles away. It was important to Sonya that they gathered with her when she returned home to mourn his death. There may also be value in seeking counseling or joining a support group.

Finally, it is important to acknowledge that others—perhaps a spouse, siblings, children or friends—share this loss. Grieve with them.

—KD

Facing Sudden Loss

The sudden, unexpected loss of someone we love can be an especially difficult experience. Loss in itself is painful enough, but sudden loss is particularly shocking. The shock intensifies our pain and our grief.

Even if on some level we understand that no one lives forever, actually losing people we love is unimaginable. When we know someone we love has a fatal disease or when we have nursed a loved one who is very ill, we have a chance to begin to prepare for the death —at least a little. However, the unexpected death of a loved one—regardless of how that loved one dies—can leave us stunned, lost, and overwhelmed with pain. We may not know where to begin to cope.

Sudden loss gives us no chance to prepare. We may feel cheated of the chance to say the last words we would have liked to say or give one final hug or kiss. Feeling cheated in this way can add to our grief, anguish, and despair.

Sudden loss can make the world feel shaky or less safe; this is a natural response to any unexpected and traumatic event. We may become fearful and uncertain, or angry and frustrated. This loss can negatively color our view of life, but hopefully only temporarily.

Sudden loss gives us three seemingly overwhelming tasks to deal with: the grief over the loss of our loved one; the sudden and unexpected absence of this special person from our daily lives; and the changes in our lives for which we did not have time to prepare. Each is a big task to take on, and each will become a part of our mourning and healing.

It helps to bear in mind that emotional pain isn't constant, and that we don't have to grieve forever. We will love forever, whether our loved ones are with us in body or not, but we do not need to grieve to honor that love. We can just love.

In talking to many people who have suffered sudden loss, I have learned that there are several important, possibly universal, ways to help move forward.

Take special care of yourself through the grief. Self-care, both physical and emotional, is important during this challenging time.

Do your mourning now. Being strong and brave is important, but I always tell those I counsel to never miss an opportunity to cry. That is not self-indulgent, but simply sensible and honest.

Expressing your feelings will help you heal. Feelings expressed disappear. Feelings repressed do not. You may need to say those words you didn't get to say, or find some other tangible way to say goodbye, even if the person you loved is no longer living.

Get support from other people. Many people who have experienced sudden loss find great help in support groups, with other people who have experienced this type of loss. You may find them through a hospice, your place of worship, or a community or social service agency. You will not only help yourself, but you may also help another and that can be a great source of strength, joy, and recovery.

Most of all, trust that the person you loved and lost would want you to remember and honor them by living a fulfilling life.

—JT

Healing After Homicide

Even though it has been over a year since our daughter was murdered, the legal case has not been resolved. I am so weary, wanting this ordeal to just be over. In my despair, I have even considered violent revenge. How do I survive what feels like is un-survivable?

"Senseless" is the unsettling description often used to describe a homicide. A murder death ranks among the most all-consuming of tragedies. What could possibly cause one human being to extinguish the life of another? There is no satisfying answer.

The devastating trauma inflicted upon the survivor can shatter the very fabric of your being. You may try to imagine how it must have been when your loved one was murdered. If only you could stop thinking about it. You try, but these thoughts may haunt you when you are awake and in your dreams when you sleep.

You may feel many stinging emotions—disbelief, anxiety, sadness, helplessness, anger, despair, and hypervigilance. The violent nature of the death could make you feel that you have lost control of your life and even your sanity. The excruciating outrage is a betrayal of a "just world" where people deserve what they get and get what they deserve.

The public nature of the death, with possible media attention, adds further complications. There may be further re-victimization if the perpetrator was not apprehended, or if caught, there was no trial or too lenient a sentence.

Under these circumstances, it is not unusual to feel hatred, bitterness, and even thoughts of revenge. You must not act upon these impulses! Share your rage with a counselor, a supportive friend, or another survivor of homicide.

There is a vast difference between "revenge" and the need for "justice." Some survivors of homicide have channeled their justifiable fury to lobby for stronger victims' rights.

Healing is a lifelong process. Understand that you are the victim and not the offender; there is no earthly reason to feel guilt or blame. As much as you may sometimes be tempted, do not build a wall around yourself; reach out to the many resources within you and around you. There are caring and compassionate family and friends, as well as therapists, homicide survivors' support groups, and state victim assistance programs.

You will survive the slow and painstaking loss and climb to a more bearable and meaningful life. Recall the consolation composed by the psalmist in his "Song of Ascents" (126:5) that has continued to echo hope for troubled souls: "They that sow in tears shall reap with songs of joy."

—EG

Loss Along the Way

"I do not understand it," Marla stated, "I lost him years ago. There even came a point when he no longer remembered me. Why do I hurt so much now?"

It was easy to understand Marla's feelings. The man she had been married to for over 50 years had developed Alzheimer's disease six years prior to his death. She had been with him for those six years, watching that slow descent. Marla described Ed as a shell of his previous self. Once open and engaging, he became guarded, even scared. He no longer recognized her or their children. "Beyond his appearance, there was nothing left of the man I married."

She grieved all those losses along the way. She cried bitterly the first day that he asked who she was. She grieved the time they went to a department store and Ed wondered if any of the photographs displayed in the picture frames were their children. She felt every moment of his decline.

It was more than just feelings. She grieved all the ways her life had changed. She mourned the loss of companionship and intimacy. She missed the walks they would take together. Marla could no longer enjoy those wonderful times when she would watch her husband play with their grandchildren.

Now she grieved Ed's death. That surprised her. She had thought that when he finally died, she would mainly feel that a burden had lifted, that it would be a relief from the constant demands of care.

She was surprised at how complex her responses were. She did feel some of that relief. Yet, there were other reactions as well. She felt guilty, remembering all the times she had lost patience with Ed, upset and angry over lapses of memory that he could not control. She also felt a sense of gratitude for all the sharing, all the better memories that bound them throughout their long years of marriage. She experienced anger. Why did this good man have to die this way? There was resentment, too, at some of the comments after his death. So many people told her she was better off, as if she had lost a wart, not a husband.

There was the loneliness, and the spare time. That surprised her. "I did so much for Ed when he was alive. That is all I did. I never seemed to have enough time. Now, the hours seem to drag endlessly."

All these responses confused Marla. Yet, all are normal, expected after long chronic illnesses. Grief is intense and complex. We grieve all the losses along the way, each change or deterioration. We never finish that grieving. At each stage of loss, even after the death, we experience new losses. They, too, have to be acknowledged. Grief is a journey. Throughout that journey, bereaved individuals need the same supplies: good listening, support, and respect.

—KD

When a Friend Dies

When I picked up my four-year-old grandson at preschool, Kenny was proud to introduce me to his new friend. Even at his young age, we begin the lifelong process of making friends. If he's lucky, he may even keep some of the friends he makes in these early years. I still have a friend who I first met in third grade.

Friends are an important part of our life. We share so much—laughter and serious conversations, people and places, active and quiet moments. Friends keep us grounded and shape our identities. They may help us find jobs, homes, or even spouses. We trust them with our secrets. Despite the important role of friends in our lives, they are often neglected in times of death. Friends are rarely mentioned in the obituary; sympathy cards are rarely sent to friends. The loss of a friend is another example of *disenfranchised grief,* the grief that results when others do not recognize our loss. In effect, we have no socially acknowledged "right to grieve" when we lose a friend. For example, no matter how close the friendship, few businesses extend time off to mourn a friend.

Yet, as friends, we do grieve. Grief is not a function of family ties or lines of descent. Grief follows attachment. When we love someone, and that person dies, we grieve.

It is important, much as we strive to support family members, that we acknowledge and recognize our own loss. We need to understand as well that each loss is different. We have unique connections and distinct meanings attached to every friendship in our lives. Some friends are part of our weekly or daily routine. We regularly speak and spend time together. The death of these friends leaves a great and obvious void.

We may have other friendships that are less intense but no less vital. While we may see them irregularly at best, they remain important in our lives. Lynn is one such friend. We talk a few times a year but she remains a critical connection in my life. She befriended me in high school, transforming my experience in what was then a large, unfriendly place.

We may find it essential to attend funerals and memorial services. The very best of these will be inclusive, clearly bringing friends to the center of the circle of mourning. When a dear colleague, Catherine Sanders died, I appreciated that the family chose three people to eulogize her—a daughter, a professional colleague, and a personal friend. I recognized the professional side of the Catherine that I knew, and was delighted that other eulogies touched on different aspects of her life. I felt very included in that ceremony.

Because all rituals are not that inclusive, we may need to find our own special ways to mourn a friend. Tom did that when his friend Mark died. He decided to go back to the ball field in the old neighborhood, a place where he and Mark shared so many good moments. There he offered a silent prayer for his friend, and quietly grieved over the loss of his longtime buddy.

Understanding the unique quality of each of our friendships helps us to appreciate our sense of loss. We can then recognize the nature of our grief.

—KD

Amanda

Patricia Loder is the Executive Director of The Compassionate Friends. Mrs. Loder became involved with TCF after her children Stephen and Stephanie died in a car accident.

A manda. She was a little thing with a big smile and a big heart. I met her on the first day of school when she accompanied Stephanie home from the bus stop. It was raining and Amanda walked Stef home so she could keep her dry under the umbrella she carried in her hand.

We had moved into the house a few weeks before school started so it was the first opportunity that Stephanie had to meet Amanda who lived up the street. Amanda was a year older than Stephanie, who was seven, but it sure didn't matter. They soon became playmates and often included Stephanie's little brother Stephen in their games and fun.

From September through March their play continued until that terrible day when the unthinkable happened. A speeding racing design motorcycle broadsided my car where my two children were seated as I attempted to turn left onto my street. It was Amanda's dad, hearing the crash, who ran down the street to help me—at the very spot Amanda and Stephanie waited for the bus. Stephanie and Stephen died as a result of the accident. Amanda lost her playmates and the world lost two beautiful children who didn't have a chance to pave their own path in the world. Stephen wasn't even old enough to wait at the bus stop with his best friends to experience school for the first time.

But Amanda didn't forget Stephanie and Stephen, and she didn't forget me. I'd walk down to the mailbox and often find that she had left me a handmade sympathy/thinking of you card. Sometimes she'd pick flowers and would leave them in the mailbox, too. I watched over her every morning as she waited for the bus—alone.

Then one day Amanda appeared at the door carrying a deck of Uno cards. "I'm lonely, and I'm pretty sure you are, too," she said, as she led me by the hand to the kitchen table. My eyes started to moisten as I sat down at the table to play. Amanda got up, hugged me tight, and whispered quietly "I miss them too." After a lingering hug she sat down and said, "Let's play!" We played several games before she finally got up and announced she had to head for home.

The cards and flowers continued to find their way into the mailbox to let me know she was thinking of me. She also continued to appear at the door with her Uno cards eager to play a game or two, or three, or four! Amanda was a comfort. When other people stopped visiting Amanda continued, Uno cards in hand. She also continued with her beautiful handmade cards and the flowers that she had so obviously picked from her mother's garden. Throughout the summer months she made her way to my house to sit and chat as we played Uno.

One day she announced, "I think I'm feeling better." I knew what she meant; it had nothing to do with being sick or under the weather. She had been missing her buddies and in our strange Uno-playing way, we were comforting each other and helping each other to grieve.

Amanda didn't come back anymore that summer but there were still the occasional cards and flowers found in the mailbox. As the first day of school rolled around the following year, I watched Amanda through the window as she walked down the street early and patiently waited for the bus to come. When she boarded that big yellow school bus she turned slightly, our eyes met, and she flashed me a big smile and waved. She knew I'd be watching over her, just as she had been watching over me, trying to fill a void, and provide comfort and love.

© Patricia Loder

When Exes Grieve

Obituaries offer insights into how dying individuals and grieving families deal with social change. I found a fascinating obituary in *The Atlanta Constitution Journal:* "Beverly leaves behind many devoted friends and colleagues and family that loved her deeply." That's standard fare. However, after the name of her surviving daughter, it read, "...and former son-in-law and ever close friend, Kenneth."

Each year, millions of individuals become divorced. Many expect divorce to be a "clean break" between spouses and family members. However, in reality, particularly when there are children, divorce does not end the relationship but changes it.

In addition to ex-spouses, each divorce creates what I call "the other ex(s)"—ex-mother/father-in-law, ex-daughter/son-in-law. Significant numbers will be saddened, stunned, or surprised by a death and by their reactions to it. "I didn't expect to feel this way" or "After all that had gone on between us…" Eventually, many wonder, "Does my grief count?"

To be sure, some discount this grief. But emotional bonds are not cleanly severed. Consider Helen, who, for the sake of her grandchildren's best interests, maintained a relationship with the first wife of her son, without his knowledge. How can you embrace grief for an ex? Give yourself permission to feel what you feel and explore those emotions.

Journal your grief. Take some time to ponder the death and the death of the relationship that preceded it. "I will always remember how [my ex]…" or "My favorite memories of [my ex] are…" Place a photograph of the ex next to your journal or computer screen to stimulate memories. Spend time letting memories tumble in your mind like clothes in a dryer.

Pay your respect. "Paying respects" is a common expectation for the need to attend a ritual. Ask yourself: In what ways can I pay respect—or create respect—for this individual and not distract "front-row" grievers?

If you feel uncomfortable, call a family member and inquire about attending either the visitation or funeral/memorial service. At a visitation or wake, you may want to attend briefly. At a funeral, you may want to slip in as the service begins and sit in the back of the chapel or funeral parlor.

Rehearse your words of condolence. Be kind and gracious. Send a sympathy card to "the family" or to specific family members. Go to the grave.

"I always take flowers," one man acknowledged, "to the grave on my ex-mother-in-law's birthday. I have missed her more than I expected."

Draw on your spirituality through acts of reflection, forgiveness, and gratitude. Write a prayer. Read it aloud. Spirituality provides the necessary courage to revisit the wounded places. Spirituality also offers resources to reinterpret, or to begin to reinterpret, elements in our loss narratives.

Writing these words has reminded me of how I received the news of the death of my ex-father-in-law. I have acknowledged that I inflicted as many wounds in that relationship as I received. I find myself praying, "Godspeed, farewell."

—HIS

Helping After a Suicide

My friend's husband recently committed suicide. I want to visit but frankly I'm scared; what can I say or do under these horrific circumstances?

Your anxiety is understandable. You ask: "What to say or to do?" Recall the aphorism: "I might not be able to stop the downpour, but I can join you for a walk in the rain."

Just being with your friend and her family is the most eloquent statement of care and concern. Bring your best self—neither prejudiced by taboos nor judgmental of the manner in which her husband died. Your conversation should be natural, genuine, and sincere. Talking is not always necessary. Accept periods of silence. A squeeze of the hand or a meaningful embrace expresses how much she means to you.

Beware of those clichés that family members of a loved one who has committed suicide often find bewildering and counterproductive.

He must have been crazy to do such a thing. Telling a family that the person was insane could trigger fear in other family members. Children often recall how they resembled the victim both physically and mentally and may begin to worry. There is no inherited gene of self-destruction.

It must have been accidental. He probably didn't mean to kill himself.

Survivors must deal with the reality of the manner of death. Even well-intentioned, unsubstantiated explanations could create further confusion and isolation. Instead of telling her how she should cope, you can encourage her to release emotions of pain and anguish. You might say: "Do you want to tell me how you're feeling? Just know if and when you feel like talking, I'm here to listen."

The loss of a loved one to suicide is an excruciating life-changing event. Just because she may be uncommunicative on one occasion doesn't signify that she may be both willing and needful at another; be sensitive to her shifting moods.

Know that actions may be more important than your words.

- Drop over with food or invite her family for dinner.
- Take the children on outings or take her out for coffee.
- Help with household chores or drive the kids to school.
- Share information about suicide support groups.

Above all, continue to demonstrate that you will continue to care, that you will never forget her and her family.

—EG

When an Animal Companion Dies

A number of years ago, I was preaching in a church. I noticed one of the older women, Elizabeth, seemed upset. After the service, she came into my office. Her dog died and she had cried throughout the week. She asked if her grief was a sign to her that something was wrong. How could she cry over an animal? I reassured Elizabeth that she was very normal. She was grieving.

We often do not think of grief when an animal dies. We imagine grief is a reaction when a person dies. If we do think of grief, we think of a child mourning the death of a beloved cat or dog. We can easily ignore or even mock the grief of an adult. The grief at the loss of an animal companion can be disenfranchised, unrecognized and unacknowledged by others. That does not mean that we do not grieve. It means that we may grieve alone without the comfort and support of others.

Grief is not just about human relationships. Grief is about attachments. For many older individuals an animal can be an important part of their lives. For Elizabeth, her dog had many roles in her life. He was a constant companion, a protector, a source of stimulation, and an impetus for exercise and conversation as she walked him.

In other cases, the animal can be a link to earlier losses. Before Pat's mother died, she asked Pat to care for her cat. When the cat died six years later, Pat felt that he had lost one more connection to his mom.

There are three keys to dealing with the loss of animal companion. The first is to recognize what we have lost. We need to think about the role that the animal played in our life. Sharing memories and understanding through remembering what we have lost is an important part of any grief. We need to look back.

Second, we need to cope with the present. We need to acknowledge our right to mourn. Like any other loss, the grief may come in waves. We may want to reach out to others who can support our loss. We may have a quiet ritual either alone or with family and friends.

Finally, we need to look to the future. We may need to decide whether we wish for future animal companionship. It is important that we make that decision and we make it for the right reasons. Well-meaning others can sometimes push us to obtain another animal as a way to avoid grief. We can no more replace an animal relationship than a human one.

Elizabeth waited a few months before she decided to bring in a new dog. She adopted an older dog from the local shelter. "We both got a reprieve," she joked. The dog was saved from the shelter; she from her grief.

—KD

Journeys through the Holidays

The Three C's of Coping with the Holidays

With the roller coaster emotions of grief, the holidays can be an especially tough time. We remember the Hanukkah that Aunt Sophia danced in the snow, the Christmas we received a bike, the Thanksgiving when the turkey was undercooked. These memories remind us of our loss.

Other reminders such as cards addressed to the person who died, holiday movies, or festive lights can make us feel out of sorts with the season. Everyone else seems so happy and joyful.

The holidays are a tough time to grieve. Knowing they will be difficult may help us understand and accept our reactions, and tap into the things we can do to help ourselves cope.

Choose. During the holidays it is easy to get involved in activities that increase our pain. But we do have choices. We can decide what activities we wish to participate in and who we want to be with. After her husband died, June was invited to join her sister-in-law for the holidays; however, the invitation actually felt more like an expectation. She decided that she would wait to choose where she wanted to be on Christmas until that morning. "I never know how much energy I'll have or how I'll feel until that day," she explained. On Christmas morning, she decided to have dinner with a few women she had met in a local widow's support group, and then go to her sister-in-law's house for dessert.

One of the choices we may want to consider is how to mark the loss during the holidays. Finding ways to recognize and acknowledge the person who has died can bring a positive focus to our grief.

Lighting a candle, creating a ritual or continuing a familiar one, placing a memento on a tree, or giving a holiday toast, are simple but meaningful ways to acknowledge the loss that is felt so keenly this time of year.

Communicate. It is important that we discuss our choices with others, especially those who are affected by them. Their ways of dealing with grief may be different. June talked with her sister-in-law, explained her feelings, and asked if she could make a decision that morning. Once her sister-in-law understood June's feelings, she was willing to be flexible. Marcy's family had to have a considerable discussion over whether or not they would have a Christmas tree after the death of one of her children, as different members of the family had different feelings

Compromise. Each of us deals with loss in our own particular way; there is no right or wrong way to grieve. When we communicate, we may find that our feelings and needs, the very ways that we cope, will differ. We need to find space for compromise. Some people in Marcy's family saw the Christmas tree as an important tribute to their late son and brother; other family members saw it as disrespectful. They talked through each point of view, and decided that this year they would have a small tree, not in the central living room, but in the family room. Those who wanted to help decorate could do so, but those who chose not to would also be respected. All could deal with their loss in their own way.

Nothing changes the fact that the holidays can be especially difficult while grieving. But as we choose our actions, communicate our choices with others, and find suitable compromises, we may find that they are bearable. And that gives us renewed strength and hope.

—KD

Grief During Passover and Easter

Each year the Jewish observance of Passover and the Christian celebration of Easter fall close to each other. While each of these religious holidays has distinct practices within its unique faith tradition, they are similar in that they are celebrations of liberation and new life. For individuals and families still grieving, the typical activities that characterize these religious holidays may be distressing. It can be helpful to anticipate how emotionally complicated these observances can be, so that expectations and plans can be realistic.

Same Seder, not the same. Since the Seder meal is at the heart of a family's annual Pesach observance, it likely will bring about powerful memories of many past Seders shared with the person who died. Just as the prophet Elijah is spiritually expected to enter to partake of the Seder, there will be strong longing for the family member no longer present. Since even otherwise non-observant Jews are likely to attend or host a Seder, this celebratory meal is a profound occasion within the family and community to reminisce about what is the same and what has changed since the last Seder. The absence of a loved one may be felt strongly, even if the griever keeps this awareness internalized and private.

The Yizkor service at the end of Passover, with its memorial prayers in synagogue and Yahrzeit candle at home, may also be a mixture of solace and sad remembrance in the midst of a holy time.

The Easter blues. The liturgical color for Easter is brilliant white, since it is a joyful celebration of resurrection and new life in Jesus. Yet the actively grieving Christian may find his or her emotional color to actually be quite "blue," with sadness overriding the themes of joy.

In addition, the 40-day period of Lent that precedes Easter has a strong focus on events leading to the death of Jesus, especially during the final week known as Holy Week. These powerful stories and images can be challenging to someone actively coping with the recent death of someone close to them. Easter Sunday is typically a time, even for those who do not go to church services, for a festive family meal; for those in mourning, such traditional gatherings can be very difficult.

No matter the faith belief, each individual and family needs to anticipate, as best they can, what is possible and desirable as the religious holidays approach. Passover and Easter offer strong messages of comfort and hope that have consoled millions over the centuries. Each tradition offers prayers, ceremonies, and customs that are known to surround grieving persons with assurance of continuity from the past to the present and into the future.

Yet those who are grieving need to realistically choose what they are able to do when it comes to the traditions of a religious holiday season. It may mean only participating in a gathering for a short time, or attending religious services only when they feel emotionally strong enough. This type of anticipatory planning can help everyone be realistic about the religious holiday. Seeking guidance from a rabbi, priest, or minister can help.

One of the blessings of a "holy day" is the opportunity to reach out to others. Many bereaved are surprised to find that their greatest solace comes in thinking of others who are also dealing with loss and sadness. Reaching out by sending a note, making a phone call, or arranging a visit may bring a real sense of holiday blessing.

—PM

When Mother's and Father's Day Heighten Loss

T he day after Grace went to her third support group meeting for bereaved parents, she called her friend, Barbara. "Oh, Barb," she said, "I think you really would have benefited from the discussion at the meeting.

"The topic for the group was how to cope with special days, like Mother's Day and Father's Day. I know those days are coming around again soon and this will be the first time for you and Mike since Sophia died."

Her friend Barbara admitted, "Mike and I have been a little anxious about these days. We'd welcome any helpful ideas that you picked up."

"Well," said Grace, "the first thing I noted was how everyone agreed that, for parents, special days like these seem to heighten the sense of loss when your child is gone. You know, sometimes I even wish they didn't print these days on the calendar; then we could just ignore them!" Barb smiled at Grace's comment; it made her feel less alone.

Grace then shared that another woman in the group said, "You know, I'm still a parent; nothing can take that away from me. Even though I really, really dislike the pain associated with my child's death, I know that I wouldn't be experiencing this grief if I hadn't loved my child. It might seem weird, but I think I should honor my grief—although I do wish such an awful loss hadn't happened."

A dad in the group then carried that thought further. "I still love my child," he said, "even though she died three years ago. It isn't just that I loved her in the past. I loved her before she was born, and I loved her while she was alive, and I still love her even now that she's gone. She isn't physically present, but she remains in my heart, my thoughts, and my prayers."

Barb then asked Grace about some of the ways that people in the group talked about how they planned to spend these special days. "Several people said that they changed their routines," said Grace. "While Mother's Day and Father's Day used to be more joyful, now they are more serious. One man goes to church and says a prayer for his child. Another person visits her daughter's gravesite. One woman makes a donation to a children's charity, while another volunteers at a childcare center."

Barb let Grace know how much she appreciated her call. "It sounds as though each of us has to do what's best for us, because each of us grieves differently," she said. "Different people do different things to cope with the challenges that arise from these special days, but we can all be proactive in deciding how to go on with our lives."

—CC & DC

Hidden Holidays

There is a considerable amount of material about how to handle grief during the holidays, specifically the winter holidays of Thanksgiving, Christmas, and Hanukkah. The material certainly is useful. These holidays can be tough for persons struggling with loss.

Yet, little is written about how to cope with those special personal days—the "hidden holidays" such as anniversaries and birthdays. In the roller coaster journey of grief, these days too may be low points, times when our grief surges.

Birthdays and anniversaries are full of memories. We may remember the surprise party that our children gave on our silver anniversary, or that special trip we took on our 50th birthday. On these occasions, the memories reinforce our experience of loss and add to the intensity of our grief.

While not filled with pleasant memories, the anniversary of the death also may be difficult. It marks a milestone—how long we have been without the person and how long we are grieving. Moreover, not just one day but many days are significant—the day she slipped into a coma, the day she died, the day of the funeral, and the day she was buried. We may center on unrealistic expectations that we should not be experiencing grief—unrealistic because the days and seasons are rife with reminders. Andy's wife died just after Labor Day. The Back-to-School and Labor Day sales remind him of that time. Some of our national holidays have somber origins, such as Memorial Day. This is our own personal memorial day.

As we deal with these hidden holidays, there are a number of things that might help. The first is simply to validate our grief, to acknowledge that this is a difficult day or time. Our feelings and reactions are natural and normal. They are the price of our relationship and our love. We need not deny them.

We need not deny these even if we know someone experiencing grief. We need not fear that we will remind them, as such days are never forgotten. A simple call, card, or note acknowledging that we are thinking of the person can mean so much. That type of support is both remembered and appreciated.

We do need to decide how to cope with these hidden holidays. Because they are likely to be difficult, we should consider what we wish to do. We cannot and should not ignore them. We cannot pretend they are simply days of the week, without meaning. We have to find a way to acknowledge that this day marks a special event in our journey with grief.

Since these days are so personal, our decisions may be very different. For Andy, anniversaries were a day to go to the cemetery. That was his special way of "being together" as they had been for so many anniversaries in the past. For Marge, birthdays and anniversaries were occasions for a memorial mass and then a small gathering shared with her family and close friends. For Lynn and Joe, her adolescent son, the anniversary of her husband's death was a time to light a candle together and share a quiet meal.

In all these situations, the people involved made careful decisions on who they wished to be with and how they wanted to acknowledge these days. Each knew that they wanted to do something special to recognize the importance of that day. That is the secret of handling those hidden holidays.

—KD

How Should We Celebrate?

It's almost Halloween and I'm not sure what to do. My husband died a few months ago. I thought I was well-prepared for his death, but now as I think about how we used to celebrate Halloween—which was also his birthday—I'm not sure what to do for my children. We always had a big celebration for him on the holiday. We all miss him terribly.

S pecial days like holidays frequently create tension and unease for bereaved families trying to manage the day with a minimum of stress. I commend you for your insight; pre-planning is more helpful then trying to ignore the day in hopes that it will go away. Whatever decisions you come to, discuss with your family so that all agree and can plan jointly. You didn't mention the ages of your children but if they are younger, you may want to continue the rituals you've done in the past by dressing them in costume and taking them trick-or-treating. Did you go trick-or-treating as a family or did you go out to eat afterwards to celebrate your husband's birthday? You might want to incorporate changes in the day's routine—visiting the cemetery before going around the neighborhood, or doing something your husband liked to do, such as taking a quiet walk in the woods or revisiting a peaceful area that was well-loved.

Think about incorporating a balloon release as part of

your day. Buy helium balloons and have the family write on the balloons with markers. The children can draw pictures or write a note to their father. Just prior to releasing the balloons, cut the string so that only a few inches remain. When the balloons are released in an open area (without trees) it's an amazing sight to see them soar. Some families read what they have written on the balloons before letting them go, others say a prayer, or talk about their feelings. Others just release the balloons all at the same time.

Acknowledging your husband's birthday and the significance of his death reinforces that his life had meaning and that he is missed. This simple, meaningful ritual can be repeated over and over and not lose its freshness.

—SS

From Attitude to Gratitude

Betsy Beard is a mother who, after the death of her only son Army Specialist Bradley Beard in 2004, found help, hope, and healing in the Tragedy Assistance Program for Survivors (TAPS). She has served as the editor of TAPS Magazine since 2008.

Weak sunlight filtering through the bare branches, a cold mist rising from the river, and frost on the ground. It's November, again. Veteran's Day comes around reminding me that my veteran didn't come home from the war. Then it's Thanksgiving and I'm supposed to be thankful...

I am drawn back in time to the first year following our son's death in Iraq. The season pressed in and I flinched away from it in anger and hurt. The holidays loomed large and bleak without Brad, and as the waves of despair and resentment washed over me, I was anything but grateful.

In the seven years between that time and now, somewhere along the road, somehow against my wishes, I began to see in a very small way that there were unexplained circumstances for which I could be slightly thankful... events that showed me that people cared, that God had not abandoned our family, that grace was still operating in the world, and that the hearts of others could still knit with ours to form new friendships and strengthen old.

With that realization, the first positive emotion that I had experienced in a very long time broke through my frozen defenses. It felt so new and so strange to me that I had to figure out what it was. I came to recognize it as gratitude. I wasn't terribly willing to acknowledge these new feelings because they seemed disloyal to Brad's memory. It felt wrong to start a sentence with "I am grateful..." But there was no way around it. Those sentences were beginning to stack up.

Through the tears, I first discovered that I was grateful to have been associated with the magnificent human being that was Specialist Bradley Beard. Even though the pain of loss was unbearable, it would have been worse never to have known him. On the heels of that revelation came gratitude for the amazing men and women of the United States Armed Forces who are willing to put their lives on the line to protect the freedoms that we take for granted.

Next, I became aware of the special people who had entered my life after Brad departed. People who willingly spent time with me in my shriveled, lifeless condition. People who went out of their way to let us know they appreciated Brad's sacrifice. Some have brought comfort or made me smile. Others have cried with me, or simply allowed me to cry in their presence. Some have listened to my angry rants. Others have prayed for me, called, or shared stories of their loved ones.

Some of us are facing losses for the first time this season. Some have been on this journey for a long time. We had no choice in the circumstances that have taken our loved ones. But we do have a choice in opening our hearts to one another as we face the difficulties of the season together.

Helpful Holiday Hints

The holidays are traditionally a time of joy and laughter, sparkle and glitter, sharing and gift giving. For people who are grieving, the holidays may be a time of mixed emotions, feelings of being overwhelmed with multiple demands, and the pain of losing loved ones. As the holidays approach, it is important to think about how you take care of yourself during this vulnerable time.

Acknowledging grief takes real work. Adjustment to the death of someone close to you does not simply come with time. The work of grief demands that you deal with all of the feelings that loss produces. This work takes emotional and physical energy that can leave you feeling like you are unable to cope with the extra demands of the holiday season.

Strive for a balanced lifestyle. With all of the parties and demands of the holidays, it is difficult for anyone to get enough rest and exercise. It is easy, and almost expected, to overindulge. Still, you should set exercise as a priority. It can alleviate depression. Learn relaxation techniques to relieve stress. Don't overdo the eggnog; alcohol often makes things worse.

Plan ahead. Sit down with your family and friends and decide those activities, experiences, and people that make the holidays special for you. Decide to do a few special things with a few special people, not everything with everybody.

Tell others clearly what you want and need. Do not be shy or embarrassed to let others know what you want in terms of emotional support, help or sharing. Unknown expectations generally go unfulfilled and lead to disappointment.

Celebrate life. It may feel impossible for someone in grief to find joy and peace at any time, yet try to accept this as your challenge. Life is worth living only to the extent that we make it so. Being a survivor means more than merely surviving a devastating experience. It means fully living.

(Based in part on materials developed by Sally Feather-stone, RN)

—EZ

Challenges on the Journey

Making Sense of Loss

We tend to think of grief as an emotional response, but grief affects us on other levels. We can experience aches and pains. We may become withdrawn, over-active, or short-tempered. We may find it hard to concentrate. All of these are ways that grief can be expressed.

One of the most difficult issues that we can face is making sense or meaning of our loss. Whenever we ask the question, "Why did this have to happen?" we are raising the issue of meaning.

Not every loss challenges our sense of meaning. Eleanor's mom died soon after she turned 96 years old. The last years had been tough. She had gradually lost her mobility, sight, and independence. "Mom had been ready to die, constantly talking about how tired she was. One night she drifted off to sleep, never to wake again." And while Eleanor misses her terribly, she never asks those "why" questions. Even in Eleanor's grief, the circumstances of her mother's death comfort her; her mother had not experienced great pain, and she seemed ready.

But other losses do challenge our sense of meaning. Tonya's husband, Phil, died soon after retiring. "We had all of these wonderful plans. He had worked so hard, but he never had time to enjoy it." Not only does Tonya struggle to find meaning in Phil's death, she has yet to find a sense of purpose in her own life now.

Mark, too, is troubled by the death of his wife. "She was such a good woman, constantly volunteering, always helping and looking out for others. Why did she suffer so?" Both Tonya and Mark remind us that struggles with meaning are likely to be more difficult when the circumstances of death are troubling or ill-timed.

Whenever we grapple with these questions, these key points may be helpful.

Remember that finding meaning or making sense of a loss is an individual process. What gives others comfort may not be helpful for us. That does not mean that we should not hear about the ways that others cope with loss; talking with others is essential to helping us find our own meaning. But we need not be troubled if we cannot find support in the thoughts that comfort them.

Search your own spirituality and beliefs. Each of us has our own way of understanding the world. That understanding is the center of our spirituality. We need to ask how our spirituality can help us make sense of the loss of our loved one.

Focus on the connections and legacies. Anyone we grieve has touched our life in some way: memories we have shared, things we have learned, new appreciations and skills we have gained. These legacies, as well as other connections we find in our own spirituality, reassure us that they still remain a part of our lives. Connections and legacies can help us find meaning even in the most difficult losses.

—KD

Who Am I?

When saddened by the death of a loved one, it is usual to think and speak of events and experiences the deceased person will miss out on. But those who are left behind in the wake of a death also think about what they, themselves, have lost. They might focus on losing the company or presence of the person who died. But they may focus on his or her role in their lives—a role like spouse or parent, breadwinner or homemaker, lover, or source of emotional stability. Whatever role the deceased person filled, it is now vacant, and this reality can be painful to those left behind.

Another important issue for those whose loved one has died is concern with their own identity. Bereaved persons may ask, "Who am I now?" For example, parents whose only child has died often ask themselves, "Am I still a parent?" In a similar way, siblings may ask themselves: "Am I still a little sister now that my brother has died?" For many of these siblings, it may be particularly difficult to explore such questions if they believe that they must now fill the roles that their brother or sister used to play or if they assume that they must suppress their grief because they have to "be strong" to support their mother or father.

A spouse who spent many of her last years of marriage caring for an ailing husband may ask "Who am I now?" The shift away from the role of caregiver may be extremely difficult, while at the same time dealing with the death of a partner.

In recent years, many who teach and write about bereavement have stressed that it is wholly appropriate to maintain continuing bonds with a loved one who has died.

Obviously, people who are left behind need to restructure their relationship with someone who is no longer physically present and when things clearly cannot be the same.

But it is quite appropriate to keep the loved one close in one's heart and mind. We can talk about them openly and recall special times shared with them. We can acknowledge that even though many things are different, they are, in a way, still with us; there is a legitimate sense to still value that role of a parent, sibling, or partner.

—CC

Managing Stress:
A Critical Grief Skill

We do not think of stress management as something we associate with grief. It sounds more necessary for someone in a high stress job, such as a stockbroker or air traffic controller. Yet, the truth is that there are few situations in life more stressful than a significant loss.

Put simply, stress is a response to change.

In loss, everything changes. Some of the changes are dramatic. Someone we love, someone we counted on, is no longer physically part of our life. There may be other significant changes as well. We may have to relocate or change our work or childcare arrangements. There may be considerable tasks associated with our loss as well. We may be burdened trying to find all the appropriate paperwork, or conflicts with other members of the family may create additional tensions.

Other changes may be subtler but no less real. Everything now seems so different, from watching television to having a meal. It is different since someone who was part of the everyday fabric of your life is now missing.

Grief is stressful. And stress can be dangerous. Stress negatively affects our health, contributing to the health difficulties often found among the bereaved.

How do we deal with the stress? The first step is to avoid any additional stress, if at all possible. We should think very carefully in these first few months, even in the first year, before making any dramatic changes in our life. This perhaps is not the best time to move or quit a job, if those situations can be avoided. In the early period of grief we may not always be thinking clearly. Each additional change we experience adds to our stress.

As much as possible, we need to "stress-proof" ourselves. A nutritious diet, adequate sleep, regular exercise, and adherence to any medical regimen are all effective ways to build our resistance to the stress inherent in grief.

We need to take stock of our lives. What events or people seem to add strain? Once we acknowledge sources of stress, we can decide how best to handle these tensions. What can we avoid or change? What simply needs to be accepted?

We also can examine the activities, events, and people that we find comforting. What has helped us deal with stress in the past? For some of us it might be prayer or meditation, massage, a walk in the woods, or simply listening to music. We need not feel guilty taking pleasure in such activities. Grief is hard work. We need time for respite, time to rest and relax from the tensions that are a normal part of grief.

In loss, we have to look at the world differently. Life is now full of problems and challenges that we never hoped or wished to encounter, maybe even challenges we never expected to face. Nonetheless, we need to remember to cultivate the strengths that will allow us to surmount even these challenges.

—KD

The Stuff of Grief

When Tracy first spoke to me, she said it was hard to cope with "the stuff of grief." I assumed she was referring to all the emotional work that is part of the journey of grief—the anger, the guilt, the loneliness, the sadness, and all the regrets. I was wrong.

Tracy was being very literal. She actually meant the stuff: her parents' possessions and clothes, the things in closets and drawers, the bits and pieces of her parents' life that bore a mute witness to her loss.

It is tough to deal with the "stuff of grief." Each time we look at it, we are reminded of our loss. Friends may tell us to get rid of it, to clear everything out lest we are constantly reminded of our grief. Others may even make requests subtly, or not so subtly, for certain items.

The first rule in dealing with the stuff of grief is that there are no rules. Each of us has to make our own decisions on what we choose to keep or what we choose to give away. As in other situations of grief, there is no one way we should cope.

Nor is there a timetable. We do not always need to tackle the stuff in the first week, months, six months, or year. We should do it when it seems right, when we are ready.

If we do decide to clear out some of the belongings, we may need to consider another question. Should we do it alone? Again, there are no rules. Some of us may need to go slowly, at our own pace, stopping at times as we confront our memories and our loss. In other families, it is simply expected that this is a task that all the siblings will share and choosing to do it alone is not an option.

Others may welcome the support and assistance of friends. This support may be especially necessary when we have no choice; some situations may mandate that we cannot use our own timetable. When Paula's mother died, Paula had only two weeks to empty out her apartment.

When and if we do it, having a system may help. My dad was a person who saved everything. The basement was full of boxes that included World War II ration books and every check he ever wrote. When we cleaned out the house, my brother, sister, and I decided to divide things into five categories. The first were things that clearly could be discarded. These items had no value to us, symbolic or otherwise. A second category was for things that we were unsure about, items we felt we should discuss as a group. A third category was simply "not now." In the midst of grief, we realized we might not always make the best decisions; we simply needed to wait. The fourth category was for things we would donate or give to other individuals, especially items we knew that my father's grandchildren and friends would treasure. The last category was for things that each of us wanted to keep for ourselves. One of the things we know about grief is that we never lose the memories; we retain the bonds even as they change in loss. Sometimes though, it is nice to have items that hold those memories. For my sister, it is Dad's old flannel shirt; wearing that shirt gives her comfort.

—*KD*

Grieving and Working

"The hardest thing I did was going back to work." But for Malik, there really was no choice. Not only did he need the income and medical coverage, he realized that he needed the activity and diversion that work offered. Malik recognized that it would do no good whatsoever to stay home focused on his loss, alone in what was once the home he had shared with his wife.

Yet, even that understanding did not make it any easier. Malik could not even pinpoint his resistance. Part of it, he acknowledged, was the difficulty of facing friends and co-workers, and those awkward moments when people did not know what to say or how to react.

Malik also knew that his own abilities were impaired now that he was grieving. He found it difficult to concentrate and felt like he was in a constant fog. What once seemed to him like meaningful work at times now seemed inconsequential. He hated the fact that he might not be the worker he once had been.

The work world is structured, full of responsibilities and expectations. Little allowance is made for the difficulties you may face as you cope with your grief. Yet, grief is a process, a roller coaster of experiences and reactions. When you do need to return to work, the following tips may be helpful.

Accept your grief. You cannot turn it off when you come to work. Recognize that as you grieve, some days may be more difficult than others. Be flexible. When you experience a rough day you may not be able to accomplish all that you wished. Be gentle with yourself.

Be gentle with others. People may not know what to say, or may not even be aware of your loss. It helps if you are clear about your loss. Share your grief with those who offer support. Co-workers and supervisors may need guidance as to the ways that they can best help.

Utilize the resources that work can offer. Human Resources or Employee Assistance programs may offer information, support, counseling, assistance, and referral. Local hospices will often sponsor grief support groups.

Take care of yourself. Grief is hard work. Adequate sleep, good nutrition, and exercise build resistance to stress. Avoid illegal drugs or alcohol; they only mask the pain of grief. Consult a physician if you have difficulty sleeping or eating. A counselor may assist if the grief inhibits your ability to function on an ongoing basis. Use whatever has helped you cope with loss and stress in your past.

There is no timetable to grief. Yet, you will likely find that as time passes that the pain lessens and you return to earlier levels of functioning, both in your personal and professional life.

—KD

Raising Children Alone

One of the challenges of being widowed at a relatively young age is raising children alone. Not only are you grieving, but now you need to deal daily with the grief of your children. A common fear is that the loss of a parent may inevitably impair your children's future.

Recent research has reaffirmed that most children can be resilient even in the face of loss. However, there are specific things that parents can do to enhance that resilience.

First, you need to take care of yourself; only if you are functioning well can you be available to your children. Examine your own response to your loss. Are you able to function in your role as parent or has the loss made you so depressed and anxious that parenting is now a difficult and unwelcome chore? If you or others have concerns that you are not functioning as well as you ought to, avail yourself of the resources you may need, whether counseling or self-help groups. In this difficult time, do not be afraid to ask your own support system, your friends and family, to lend a hand. Grieving children benefit from knowing that they can count on the support of a network of adults.

Helping your children does not mean that you need to hide your grief. Instead, you need to model it, explaining what you are experiencing and how you are coping with your reactions. Toni does that. In moments when memories overwhelm her, she tells her children, "I was just thinking about the time Dad took us on that skiing trip." As she shares both her own tears and her own laughter, her children know it is safe to share theirs.

The key here is sharing grief. Yet, in that sharing it is still important to remember you are the parent. It is important to accept your children's' expressions of grief. There is danger, however, in transgressing those critical boundaries between parent and child. Your children always need to know you are taking care of them and protecting them; you are in charge. Children need their surviving parent now more than ever. While you may share your feelings and reactions, it is important not to overwhelm children with your fears.

Children need information and reassurance, and their questions should be answered in honest ways appropriate to their age. They may need reassurance that they did not cause the death, and that they are safe and will be cared for by adults they trust. For Tommy, the sudden death of his mom made him anxious that something might happen to his dad. When he asked his dad the "what ifs," his dad would simply dismiss his questions. Finally, his dad seriously addressed his concern, reassuring Tommy that the condition that affected his mother was unlikely to reoccur and that his aunt and uncle would always be there to take care of him if needed.

Children also need consistency. Try as much as possible to keep consistent routines and discipline. The loss of a parent is a significant and critical change. The fewer other changes a child experiences, the less stress they encounter and the more reassured they will feel. When changes are inevitable, involve the child in a meaningful way.

Children thrive on the warmth and unconditional love of their parents, whether coping with loss or coping with life.

—KD

Helping a Child Deal with Death

What can an adult say to a child following the death of a be-loved family member or friend? Children often ask probing or painful questions. For a grieving adult, it may seem daunting to have to explain death to a child, especially when there are no simple answers. The following guidelines may make this process easier.

It is okay to say you don't know the answer to a child's question. You can even say, "No one knows for sure, but this is what I think."

Consider a child's age and ability to understand complex ideas. Many experts believe children do not have a mature understanding of death until about age eight or nine. Younger children may think that being dead is temporary, and that the dead person will return in the future.

Use precise terms when talking about death. People typically re-fer to "losing" a loved one. Children may interpret this literally and assume that the person can be found. You should also explain that being dead means that the body has stopped working and that it can-not be fixed. It no longer feels cold or gets hungry, and it does not feel any more hurt or pain.

If the child asks whether you will die, respond that everybody dies someday, but that you hope to live to do things with the family for a long time.

Remember that children cannot tolerate long periods of sadness; they may want to play and participate in their usual activities. This does not mean that they didn't love the person who died, nor does it mean that they are being disrespectful. It is okay to permit or encourage children to have fun like they did before the death.

Changes in the child's behavior or patterns might be signs that the child is experiencing problems associated with the death. In these instances, it's appropriate to obtain advice from a specialist in child bereavement counseling.

Many school-age children benefit by participating in bereavement groups with other children who have suffered losses. Children hate to be different from their peers; in a group, they discover they are not alone.

Although you may not know what to say, don't avoid bereaved children. Tell them that you love them and, although you may be sad or crying, you will always love and take care of them.

—NBW

Yearning and Searching

After the death of her husband, Samantha found herself reaching out in what seemed like an attempt to make contact with him. Sometimes she found herself setting a place for him at the table or waiting for him to come up the driveway at the end of the day. On other occasions, she thought she had caught a glimpse of him in a crowd at the mall or heard his voice from the next aisle in the grocery store.

It wasn't as if Samantha didn't know that her husband had died, especially since his death had occurred quickly and without warning. To her, it was a cosmic slap in the face. Even though she knew he was dead, she couldn't help "reaching out" to him in ways that surprised her.

Professionals call what is happening to Samantha and to many other bereaved persons experiences of "yearning" and "searching." People yearn for the lives they once had, and for the comfort and presence of those they love who are no longer there. They want to hold on to the past and wish it was still part of their present.

Yearnings like this can lead people to search for that past and for the absent loved one. For the most part, they don't do this deliberately; it's just that they find it so hard to give up the way things used to be. There is a part of them that desperately wants to hold on to the past, a part that (almost) believes they could do it if they could just search out and rediscover the person they love and the way of life they once enjoyed.

Professionals think of yearning and searching as a form of "reality testing." When bereaved persons test to see what is truly real, often over and over again, they are engaged in a process of rediscovering the world. Or, they are discovering what the world no longer is and what it is now really like.

It is a world in which their loved one is no longer present as before. It is a world in which the life they once had is forever and irreversibly altered. These are hard facts to face and aren't likely to be absorbed all at once.

But facts like this need to be faced. They are real, after all. In truth, all any bereaved person can do is adjust his or her inner, psychic world to the realities of the outer, objective world.

This doesn't have to be done all at once, like gulping down a bitter pill. It might help to confront this reality a bit at a time, like when one gradually swallows an unpleasant medicine.

For some, adjusting to new realities after a death may go on for a long time, perhaps even for the remainder of their lives. For others, the process may be shorter, gentler, or quicker.

Reaching out for someone who is no longer there isn't bad in itself. It's part of a larger process of coping with loss and adapting to a new situation in which all bereaved persons find themselves after the death of someone they love.

A lesson from the previously bereaved is to take this process of "reaching out" for what it is and not to confuse it with something magical that really might restore the much-loved past in the new present.

—*CC*

The Dumb Things People Say

A s if dealing with the loss of someone we love is not bad enough, we also may have to deal with the sometimes thoughtless things people might say to us as we grieve.

Many of these fall into the category of "false cheer" or "the silver lining"—comments like: *You are young. You will marry again. It was his (or her) time. Everything always happens for the best.*

At best, these comments are insensitive. At worst, they can be destructive, corroding our relationships or alienating us from seeking support from others.

Erin Linn, in a wonderful book titled *I Know Just How You Feel: Avoiding the Clichés of Grief,* (Pubs Mark, 1986), offers three helpful questions for dealing with insensitive remarks.

What was the person trying to say? Friends and family are not intentionally cruel. In most cases, they are trying to convey support and comfort. When we ask this question, we recognize the goodness of their intentions even as we understand that their expression of support was poorly chosen.

Why did the comment hurt? Only by understanding why the comment troubled us can we begin to heal that hurt. Most of these comments hurt because they invalidate our grief. Whether we will marry again does nothing to resolve the sense of grief we may have at present; we will always mourn the loss of our mate.

What can we say? We may never have the opportunity to respond, but just thinking about what we could have said reaffirms a sense of control and empowers us not to be a victim again. We can answer comments like *At least you have other children* with a simple *It is a great comfort to have them, but I will always miss Jan.* A reply to *Everything always happens for the best* might be *I will never understand how the loss of my mother could be for the best.* Responses such as these reaffirm our grief and, perhaps in the most favorable situations, teach others how to be more supportive.

Other troubling comments may take the form of unsolicited advice. *You need to get rid of all his clothes right now* or *You should just stay busy, and maybe start dating again.* In such situations, it is helpful to remember two points.

Trust our own instincts. Each of us handles our loss differently. What worked for someone else may not work for everyone. We need not move the clothes at all. If they are troubling us, we may want to move them to the attic until we can carefully decide.

Give ourselves time and space. In the beginning, we might not know what it is we want or what we should do. While it may be important to not become isolated, we might not have the energy to keep up with social activities, much less consider dating again. Most grieving people have noted that there is no need to rush anything that doesn't feel right.

The best support in grief is often the quietest. It need not say much beyond *I am sorry* or *How can I help?* Support may appear in caring actions—the meal that is delivered or the chore that is done without asking.

At the funeral of her husband, Joan's neighbor pressed a key into her hand. "It will be lonely sometimes," the neighbor shared. "There will be times you may not want to be alone. You have my key. Come over." That level of quiet caring is always welcome.

—KD

The Different Ways We Grieve

When her daughter died, Lynette constantly found herself crying. The slightest reminder of her daughter, even an ad in a magazine reminiscent of a dress her daughter wore, would cause Lynette to dissolve in tears. Her husband, Rob, on the other hand, was very involved in a scholarship fund set up in their daughter's name. Lynette never saw him cry. She began to wonder if Rob even ever loved their child, or if he was even grieving.

We grieve in very different and individual ways. Rabbi Earl Grollman, a mentor and former associate editor of the newsletter *Journeys,* reminded us that grief was like snowflakes or fingerprints; each person's grief is both personal and unique.

Some of us grieve in a way more like Lynette. Grief can be a highly emotional experience, sweeping over us like waves. We may feel many, even contradictory, emotions such as anger, guilt, loneliness, sadness, or pining for the person who died. Our expression of grief mirrors these inner feelings; we cry, rage, or withdraw. We may find it helpful to express and explore these emotions.

Others of us may grieve in a way more like Rob, with less intense emotions. Rather than the vivid emotional colors of Lynette, our emotions may come through more muted, like pastels. We may express our grief in a more cognitive way, thinking about the person often. We may find it helpful to do things for our grief such as managing a scholarship fund or being involved in another activity. For example, the founders of Mothers against Drunk Driving (MADD) used their grief over the deaths of their children to lobby for stricter laws that changed the way society viewed drinking and driving.

These different ways or patterns of grief are just that. They are different. No pattern is better or worse. They are simply expressions of the fact that we cope with loss in our own way.

They become problems when we insist that someone grieve in our way or fail to acknowledge that we handle our losses differently. For Lynette, it was helpful to understand that Rob's interest in the scholarship fund was something he was doing for his daughter. It was his way to express love and to leave an enduring legacy to their daughter's achievements. They realized that their differences in grieving styles were simply that, and not differences in the love they shared for their daughter.

Other times, we may fail to give someone the support they need. Sue's mother lived with her and her husband Gary. In their busy professional lives, Sue's mother served as a nanny to their children. For nearly 12 years, she lived with them, making their morning coffee and helping keep their house in order. When she died, Sue tearfully recounted that she never even learned how to use their new coffee machine. Gary cheerfully began to show her how.

He had missed the point. Sue was not dealing with a problem, but a feeling. Without her mother, she now felt so alone.

We can benefit from our different, complementary ways of coping. When Tony's dad died, Tony was tearful and upset. He later shared how much he appreciated his wife's attitude. "Maria did everything—arranged transportation, picked out my clothes, even arranged for flowers. She let me just grieve." Our different grieving styles do not need to be a source of conflict. They can be a source of strength.

—KD

Mixed Memories

"Everyone says hold on to the good memories, but what do you do when the memories are bad?" Carol once raised this question to a group. Her spouse had died, ending a marriage that had been fraught with conflict, verbal abuse, and separations.

She brought up a critical issue—memories that sustain many in grief are not always available for everyone. For some, the memories are not good.

This may not always follow years of conflict. Paul had a good relationship with his wife. They were married over forty years, and he described them as "mostly happy." Then his wife developed a slow degenerative disease. During that time, Paul's caregiving demands increased as his wife's condition declined. His wife became increasingly frustrated over her incapacities and they began to argue a great deal. "Whenever I think of Lisa," Paul confessed, "I cannot get past those last terrible years."

Nor are these bad memories restricted to spouses. Craig and Bea's son, Tyler, spent much of his teenage and young adult years in seemingly perpetual battles with his parents. Disobedient, he was in constant trouble with school and then the law. He spent years in juvenile detention, rehabilitation programs, and prison. To Craig and Bea, the good memories of his first few years were crowded out by constant crisis and conflict

These ambivalent and conflicted relationships can complicate grief in many ways. In such cases, individuals grieve not only what they lost, but also what they never had. They may grieve over the fact the relationship could have been better. They may struggle with difficult feelings of anger and guilt.

There may be unfinished business, things one would have wished to say or regretted saying. This, too, complicates grief.

The death can resurrect all the old conflicts and feelings, at a time when energies are already limited by being involved in grief.

Social support may be more limited. Others may not know what to say or how to respond, even questioning, given the conflict, why the person would mourn the loss.

In such cases, it is essential to remember that one does, in fact, need to grieve such losses. One has no choice. Individuals grieve the loss of attachments no matter how negative these attachments may have been.

Some self-help activities may be useful. Paul, for example, found solace in putting together a picture album of his life with Lisa. As he reflected on the photographs, deciding which ones to place in the album, he was reminded of the earlier years of his marriage. Craig and Bea both wrote long letters to their son, expressing their love, frustration, feelings of powerlessness, and their wishes that things might have been different.

When relationships are complicated and memories are bad, counseling can be useful. The journey of grief is hard enough, particularly when the terrain is difficult. One need not go it alone.

—KD

A Lost Soul

A *lost soul* was my dad's description of someone who seemed down and directionless. I have met many such lost souls while counseling individuals grieving a significant loss. When we grieve we may experience intense emotions, find ourselves disoriented and unable to concentrate, or see that we are not behaving as we usually do. We may find that we feel physically ill, experiencing a variety of aches and pains, or we may just be lethargic. And grief also can affect our sense of spirituality.

Both Maria and Terri were just such lost souls.

Throughout her young husband's bout with cancer, Maria fervently prayed for his recovery. Even while he was in hospice care, Maria still hoped for a miracle. When he died, a part of Maria's faith died with him.

Terri's spirituality was less centered on God and more on a general belief that "what goes around, comes around." When her daughter was killed in a car crash, Terri could not believe why she should have suffered so. Terri questioned what she or her daughter had done to deserve such a fate.

Whatever our spirituality, losses can really test our beliefs. One of the issues in grief is to reconnect, maybe even rebuild, a faith or a philosophy challenged by loss.

Sometimes that means looking at our faith in a much deeper way. Most religions have long encountered death and loss. They speak to human tragedy in complex ways. We might like to simplify those beliefs.

For example, Maria realized that while she never could understand why her beloved husband had to die so young, she could still find strength in her faith. She acknowledged that somehow she had strength greater than she imagined as she raised her young son alone. Perhaps that was an answer to a prayer. She found comfort in the rituals her church offered during her husband's illness, at the time of his death, during the funeral, and after. Maria felt supported by her faith community whether in visits by her pastor and ministry team, kindnesses by other church members, or a grief support group offered through her church.

Other times we may have to look deeper inside ourselves, examining, perhaps even modifying, our beliefs. Terri had to realize the world was not as fair and just as she once believed.

As we struggle with our spirituality after a loss, we can use the resources of our faith. Every form of spirituality, each faith, has books and teachers to turn to as we try to make sense of our loss. There also may be rituals that offer comfort and assist our search for meaning. And, like Maria, we certainly can look to support from our faith community, whatever our religion or beliefs.

We need not do this by ourselves. The inherent nature of spirituality reminds us that however we define our sense of spirituality, we are connected—we are not alone.

—KD

Continuing Bonds—or Chains?

Dorothy married relatively late in life. At 47, she was an extremely independent woman when she married Steven, a man in his 60s. Steven had strong beliefs, including that women should not drive. Dorothy, though she had a driver's license for nearly 30 years, gave up driving. Having been independent for so long, she relished the care that Steven lovingly provided. She enjoyed being chauffeured everywhere, whether working, shopping, or doing chores. When Steven died, however, she refused to resume driving. He would not like to see her drive. Her decision severely limited her mobility in her suburban town.

Will was 13 when his dad died. Will's dad was a minister from a long line of clergy; Will's last promise to his father was to enter the ministry. When he was a senior in college, the prospect of seminary held a sense of dread. Yet, every time he raised questions, his paternal grandmother reminded him of the promise he made to his dying dad.

The fact is that we always continue a bond with the person who died. The people we loved remain in our memories. We retain the legacies they left us and the life lessons taught; they are part of our biographies. We need not give up those connections even in death.

Yet, some of the bonds may not be healthy. Sometimes the ties that bind us are more like chains, imprisoning us in a past life that now has limited relevance. For Dorothy, whatever choices she made when Steven was alive have little relevance now that he has died. And clearly it is unfair to Will to enter a life he no longer seeks because of a promise made as a young adolescent.

How can we tell if the bonds we have to the person who died are treasures to carry in our journey or burdens that belabor us? As we ponder these ties, we should ask ourselves two questions.

Does our connection acknowledge our loss? One of my students told me that her grandmother set a plate for her late husband every night. The student asked if that was healthy. My response—*Does she put food on it?*—drew a laugh, but the question was serious. It is one thing to symbolically acknowledge a presence; it is another to expect that the food will be eaten. In Dorothy's case, her failure to drive demonstrates her difficulty acknowledging the changes in her life after Steven's death.

Does the connection allow for continued growth? The question reaffirms the need for our continued development even as we face loss. Dorothy's failure to drive will severely limit her opportunities for growth. Will's promise to his father does not allow him to pursue his own dreams.

As we answer these questions, we can make choices about the legacies and promises we wish to carry and those we wish to leave. For Dorothy, it was recognition that what worked when Steven was alive is no longer viable. For Will, it was understanding that ministry could be understood in many ways, and that the best legacy he could give his dad was to serve his God in a way compatible with his own talents and interest.

As we journey with grief, it is important to acknowledge the ties we will always keep with the person who died. Yet, it is equally important that these ties not bind us to a past that impairs our present and future.

—KD

All My Losses

Marie indicated it was not just one loss that had brought her to counseling but "all those losses." In the past year, her husband, sister, and closest friend had died. An older brother was now ill, his prognosis uncertain. After Marie was in a car accident, she reluctantly, at the request of her children, stopped driving as her arthritis made it somewhat difficult to react quickly.

Marie's situation is not unique. As we move into later life, we often experience multiple losses. The writer Muriel Sparks once had one of her older characters note that "we live amongst a battlefield along with the dying and dead." At times we experience losses, both tangible and intangible, seemingly cascading into our life.

Yet while age increases the frequency of loss, strength and wisdom also comes with later life. We have experienced loss before, so grief is not unknown to us; we know of its ups and downs, the surges of grief as we approach holidays and special events. We have lived with the emotional and physical pain, the confusion, and the spiritual doubts. Grief is probably not the stranger it was when we were young.

As we age, we acknowledge our mortality. However painful, loss is no longer the surprise it was when we were younger, and we live among other survivors who can offer empathy and support.

We still need to take care of ourselves as we grieve, starting with good self-care. As we age we become more vulnerable to the inevitable stress and life changes that come with loss. Eating well, getting physical activity, and adequate rest can help give us the strength to handle our grief. In addition, we need to avoid self-destructive habits such as the dangerous use of alcohol or abuse of medication.

We should take advantage of whatever resources we have developed over the years. These can be internal resources such as the faith or philosophy that has sustained us up to this point. It can also include our external strengths such as friends and family that we have nurtured and that nurtures us even now.

It may very well be that we may have outlived much of our support system or that the people we count on are overwhelmed by their own losses. In such cases, other support is available—through support groups sponsored by hospices, funeral homes, churches, synagogues, or senior centers. If grief has led to self-destructive behaviors or depression, or is keeping us from participating in our daily activities, it may be helpful to speak to our physician or to a grief counselor.

With age comes a sense of perspective and wisdom. It is always wise to know our limits and to seek help when we need it.

—KD

Grief Can Be Complicated

M ost people experiencing a loss will grieve. During this time, they may react to a loss in many ways—emotionally, physically and spiritually, in the ways they think and behave. Many experience grief as a roller coaster of reactions, full of ups and downs, highs and lows, days when they feel better, and days when they do not feel so well. These dips tend to be more pronounced in the first year and a half. Over time, they diminish.

There is no timetable, though, for grief. In working with bereaved persons, I ask specific questions after the first tough period of about 18 months. The questions are based on the fact that the bereaved will still feel those cycles of highs and lows. I ask: Do those lows come often? Are they less intense? Do they last long? Some people will experience no lessening of these highs and lows. These people may experience what can be called "complicated mourning."

Mourning can become complicated for many reasons. In some cases the complicating factors are relationships that are extremely close, dependent, or full of mixed feelings. In other cases, the circumstances of the death are troubling, such as sudden, traumatic, or violent death. Just as each grief reaction is different for many reasons, the reasons for complicated mourning can differ.

There are many types of complicated mourning. In the **chronic pattern,** the roller coaster never seems to diminish. Grief never seems to end. Denise's grief is like that. Even though it has been five years since her husband's death, she cries daily and finds no joy in living.

In **exaggerated grief reactions,** one or two reactions are expressed in an extreme way. For example, anger is a natural and normal reaction to loss. But a violent rage, expressed in destructive acts against others or oneself, would illustrate exaggerated grief.

Delayed grief reactions are often experienced by people who become focused on taking care of the needs of others in a time of loss. Their own grief is never expressed. Later, sometimes years later, some event may trigger this unresolved grief. This happened to Margaret. When her mother died she was only 29 and was busy taking care of her father and her young children; she never grieved herself. When she turned 52, a year older than her mother had been when she died, she began to really grieve her mother's early death.

In **converted** or **masked grief reactions,** grief is hidden by another problem. This may include problematic behavior, such as drinking or taking drugs. Mark rarely drank when his wife was alive. Now a widower, he began to drink heavily to forget the pain. The grief is still there but now he struggles with alcoholism as well. In other situations people can experience their grief through physical aches and pains.

This brief article barely touches the surface of complicated mourning. If someone, after about one and one half years, really feels that those lows are no less frequent, intense, nor diminished, it might be helpful to see a grief counselor. The counselor will help discover what it is that seems to be complicating grief. And more importantly, the counselor can help find the resources necessary for healing.

—KD

When Do I Seek Professional Help?

G rief generally can affect us in a lot of different ways—physically, emotionally, spiritually—as well as in the ways we behave or think. While it is normal to be out of sorts when we are grieving, certain manifestations of grief should be evaluated and treated by professionals. Here are some "yellow lights" that might be cautionary signals.

Physical reactions. While physical manifestations of grief such as fatigue, aches, and pains may very well be related to the stress we experience in grief, any persistent physical complaints ought to be evaluated by a physician. Make your physician aware that you are grieving a significant loss.

Grief that is disabling. Seek counseling if grief is critically interfering with key roles in work, school, or at home, especially if you cannot seem to minimally function in those roles.

Extreme anxiety or sadness. While anxiety and sadness are normal reactions to loss, seek help if they seem severe or disabling. If you have a history of anxiety or depression, it might be worthwhile to be proactive and seek help.

An intense inability to speak of the person who died or an extreme unwillingness to make any changes in his or her room. If these or other minor events trigger intense reactions, they may not signal complicated grief but should still be evaluated.

Destructive behaviors. While anger is a natural part of grief, intense anger or thoughts of hurting others should be a sign to seek hclp.

Self-destructive behaviors. Thoughts of suicide, excessive drinking, or excessive use of dependence upon prescription medications or illegal drugs, are signs that one should seek immediate help.

If you feel you need to speak to a counselor, you should do so.

The Association for Death Education and Counseling (ADEC) maintains a list of counselors certified in grief counseling (www.adec.org).

—KD

Taking Care of Yourself

After an important loss in their lives, bereaved people are often told, "Take care of yourself." But what does that mean? Sometimes it may mean taking care of basic physical needs, such as eating and drinking, exercise, and sleep. After a loved one has died, especially after a long illness, it can be very hard to redirect focus from taking care of a loved one to taking care of yourself.

Hydration. Hydration is an essential and sometimes overlooked need for healthy adults, but if you are grieving, you may not think about being thirsty. A minimal intake of fluids, reliance on beverages that are high in caffeine and sugar, and constant crying can all contribute to dehydration.

A different problem may occur for some who try to minimize their grief by drinking too many alcoholic beverages. In addition to dehydration, relying on alcohol to cope with grief can be self-destructive in other ways.

By turning away from excessive amounts of alcohol, caffeinated beverages, and sodas with high sugar content, you could avoid doing further harm, settle jangled nerves, and minimize insomnia.

Nutrition. In order to cope with loss we all need the energy provided by nutritious food. A well-balanced diet, one that emphasizes foods like fruits, vegetables, and whole grains, will be a better choice to maintain the energy you need, rather than the excess calories, fat, and sugar so typical of most comfort foods and fast foods. A good way for friends to help is to ask them to pick up extra salads, whole grain breads, hearty soups, and fruit for us.

Good nutrition is essential to taking care of ourselves and going on with our lives, while remembering that it's okay to allow ourselves a small treat once and awhile.

Rest. For most of us, rest and good sleep recharge our batteries and prepare us to face the challenges of each day. Unfortunately, many bereaved people find it difficult to get a good night's rest when they need it most. Increased consumption of caffeine and alcohol can add to this problem.

For most people, it is a mistake to smother one's honest reactions to loss with sedatives or painkillers. But in some cases, when lack of sleep is interfering with the ability to function, it may be helpful to use sleeping pills on a temporary basis. Check with your physician or pharmacist even if you decide to use an over-the-counter sleep aid, and be sure to share that your sleeplessness may be tied to your loss.

Exercise. Exercise can help bereaved people refocus their thoughts and redirect their energies, even if only for a little while. Exercise helps you just get out of the house and have a change of scene. That can help with the tendency in many bereaved persons to retreat from life.

Exercise can be as simple as taking a walk or a jog, swimming, or using a workout DVD at home. Some physical activities can include friends, such as tennis or golf.

Grief affects us physically; it's important that we help take care of ourselves in healthful ways.

—CC & DC

Help for the Journey

Evaluating Advice
for the Grieving

In the midst of grief, we receive the advice of others. Sometimes it is solicited, from family, friends, or co-workers; other times it is simply offered. We may even seek out advice, eagerly reading an article in the paper, or surfing the Internet for information.

But we may be torn by conflicting suggestions—one person may advise tossing out all reminders and cleaning the closets while another recommends that we go slowly. How do we make sense of the conflicting advice?

Grief is an individual experience. We no longer look at grief as a predictable set of stages. Rather, we view grief as a highly individual process influenced by many factors such as our relationships with the person who died, the ways that we cope, and the nature of the death, as well as a range of other factors. Some of us may respond to a death with deep emotion; others may find that grief affects us in other ways. We should be suspicious of any advice that tells us how we should feel and how we should grieve.

One size does not fit all. Since grief is a highly individual process, it follows that we may find support and solace in different ways. In my support group, I emphasize that we can tell what helped us rather than what would help another. Support groups can be highly useful in validating grief, offering suggestions as we cope with loss, and extending hope in a difficult time. Yet, support groups are not necessarily for everyone. Some may have adequate support among their circle of friends. Others may find more private ways to cope.

There is no timetable to grief. Grief is like a roller coaster—full of ups and downs, highs and lows. Like a roller coaster, for many of us, the early part of the journey may not be the most difficult; the shock of the loss and the support of friends cushion us. Generally, most of us resume prior roles. Yet if we are not functioning in our major roles—work, school, or home—or if we are resorting to drugs or alcohol to cope, it may be time to seek additional help. And even though there is no specific timetable to grief, if over a period of time, maybe even a year or two, we experience the lows as often and intensely as ever, we may also want to seek professional assistance.

Say goodbye to closure. We never get over a loss. We learn to live with it. For most of us, pain lessens over time and we function at least as we did prior to the loss. Yet, even years later, we may deeply miss the person who died. When my first grandchild was born, I missed sharing it with my parents, even though they had died a decade earlier. Distrust any counsel that suggests or promises that elusive closure.

We can trust ourselves. Perhaps our inner voice is our best source of advice. What has helped us in the past? This can be good counsel for the present. Moreover, as we hear the recommendations of others, we can ask this question: *It may have worked for others, but does it sound right for me?* We are likely to know that answer.

—*KD*

Finding the Right Help

Grieving is an intensely personal experience, but we cannot do it alone. Shortly after the death, people send cards, bring food, offer condolences, and come to the viewing or the funeral.

You want and need special people who will stand beside you as you struggle through the weeks and months following the death of a loved one. You want someone who will understand what you are experiencing, someone who will be patient with your slowness to snap back to your old self. If your struggle is extreme, however—if you are having trouble eating or sleeping or if you feel overwhelmed by the adjustment—you may want to contact someone with professional experience in coping with grief.

You need to find someone who can best provide the help you need. You need the kind of helper who understands what it is to grieve and who will be willing to hear what you are going through without judging you. You'll want someone who doesn't shower you with "pat answers" and clichés. An effective helper will take the time to be with you as you slowly move through your grieving.

How do you go about finding such a helper? In many instances people will turn to a good friend, a close family member, or their pastor, priest, or rabbi. These helpers can provide an opportunity for you to release some of your strong feelings into words. They will support you as you work your way back into your regular daily activities. While you will want someone who knows what it is to grieve, it is best not to turn to someone who is mourning a recent death. That person has his or her own grief work to do and may not be able to respond helpfully to your needs. Most hospices wait until people have mourned for at least a year before accepting them as volunteers.

If you need special help because you are feeling stuck in the grieving process, do not hesitate to seek professional grief counseling. If, some months after the death of your loved one, you are still grieving the way you were right after the death—if you are still feeling overwhelming sadness, if you are still having difficulty sleeping, if you can't make decisions or just "can't get going" every morning—you may want to talk with an experienced counselor.

To locate such a helper in your community you might ask the bereavement worker at a local hospice for the names of grief counselors; your family physician may also be a good resource.

If you are part of a faith community, it is natural to turn to your clergy person. But you need to know whether that person has the patience or the time to work with you over an extended period. How does one know if a particular member of the clergy is also a competent counselor for this situation? The most highly trained clergy will usually be members of one of the following professional organizations: The Association for Death Education and Counseling, The American Association of Pastoral Counselors, The Association of Clinical Pastoral Education, or The American Association for Marriage and Family Therapy. If your own minister does not have special training in dealing with grief, he or she should be happy to refer you to a colleague with such training.

It is a sign of strength to seek out a helper. It means you are ready to move forward and will take the steps to grow through your grief.

—PI

Should I Go to a Support Group?

When I counsel bereaved people, they frequently ask if I think they would benefit from a support group. I answer the question with one of my own: "What do you expect to gain?"

Support groups are a time-tested method of help for people struggling with all sorts of difficulties. They have evolved from a model that sought to inhibit certain behaviors, such as drinking, to groups that try to enhance and support individuals as they adapt to life issues.

Groups are not magic. There are no words that can be uttered within a group setting that can make grief disappear. Groups are places to work together to support one another; they are places where one gives as one takes. This is very important, because sometimes individuals can be so needy in their loss that they have nothing to give. In such cases, individual counseling may be the best approach.

Not everyone will find a support group suitable; each individual grieves in his or her own way. For many, however, support groups have much to offer. One thing they can provide is validation. Grief can be so isolating. One is besieged by so many reactions: physical, emotional, and spiritual. One needs a place to recognize that these reactions are part of the journey of grief. In counseling, I am sometimes asked, "Am I going crazy?" Support groups reaffirm that one is not going crazy; one is grieving.

While every loss is unique, through support groups one can bask in the support of others who have some basis of empathy. They have experienced loss. They understand. They know.

Groups provide some time away. For many people, their support group can be a break in the loneliness and the boredom that often comes with grief.

Support groups offer suggestions for coping with daily difficulties of grief. There is no one solution to dealing with loss; however, support groups can offer a range of alternatives. By listening to stories of how others coped with a particular problem, one can find the solution that might work best.

Support groups offer two other gifts. They provide hope by providing models that reaffirm that one can survive loss. Also, they reaffirm that in helping others, one helps oneself. Even in the midst of grief, one can find new empathy, new understandings, and renewed strengths.

—KD

The Whole Exhausting Thing

Elizabeth Uppman is a freelance writer and mother of two. She lives in Overland Park, KS, and is currently working on a memoir.

*I*t was time to begin. The facilitator suggested we break the ice by saying our names and the names of our loss. I expected to have the most tragic story—a little boy, three years old, disability and illness, a year in hospice, pneumonia, death. I expected my story to overwhelm them.

But everybody else had an overwhelming story, too. One couple found their four-year-old dead in her bed one morning, her heart damaged by a rare virus. One couple's little boy drowned in a swimming pool not ten feet from his father. One woman's son died in bed of a heart attack, leaving her to raise her two teenage grandsons. And on and on and on.

These stories, all from folks who had found the strength to drive here and face a roomful of strangers—these stories should have squeezed some sympathy out of me. They didn't. As each parent spoke of a lost child, I knew each loss was unbearable, but I couldn't respond to it; I didn't feel it inside my rib cage. My rib cage was full. The loss of my little boy was too fresh to allow in any more loss.

Still, I listened—who couldn't?—and I remembered to say what was required: "I'm sorry" and "That must have been terrible," and "I'm sorry" again. Though I didn't connect emotionally with these people, I respected them for what they'd gone through. I couldn't treat their losses casually, the way outsiders sometimes treated mine.

When everyone returned the next week, I wondered what was left to talk about. How many times can you say, "He died and I can't stand my life anymore?" The facilitator gently teased us out and we had a stumbling conversation. It was painful and awkward.

As the weeks wore on, I sometimes thought it odd that almost everyone attended the meetings, and yet the meetings were often more silence than talk. Did it help people to sit in a room staring at other people staring back at them? Did it help me? I didn't often break those silences—I didn't want to cry in front of everyone or bore them or share too much of my precious, private store of feelings—but I usually left the place angry that I hadn't gotten to say what I wanted. In the car on the way home, I rehearsed what I should have said. My emotions seemed thicker and more difficult after a meeting, more stirred-up. The whole thing was exhausting.

But just when I'd be thinking, once again, that this was a big waste of time, one of the other parents would tell a gripping story. The parents whose little girl died in her sleep described the police arriving at their house the night of her death, suspicious, looking for signs of abuse or neglect, and I felt horrified for them, heartsick for them. The mother who lost her adult son found an undeveloped roll of film among her son's things, and I felt her mixture of dread and wonder as she described looking at those pictures for the first time. These stories made me wish for a way to hope on behalf of another person, as if my hope could spark some hope in them, like a chain reaction.

After those meetings, I didn't feel angry. Something big and clear, something quiet and humane, stepped through my grief, blocking me out and creating a little space for someone else.

Using Our Support System Well

When facing grief and loss, we need the support of others. Even for those with support there is a difference between *having* support—that is, having family and friends around us willing to help—and effectively *receiving* the support we need. Sometimes we do not use our support systems well. Here are some tips for receiving effective support.

Make a list of all the people you count on. Ask yourself these questions: *Are all my friends and neighbors included? Am I involved in a faith community or any groups? Did I include children?* Even children and adolescents can offer support.

People are often surprised by the size of the list that emerges. That task itself helps by reminding us that we are neither isolated nor alone as we face a loss.

Place a "D" next to all the people on the list who are *doers*. These are the people in our lives who are always willing to help. In times when our own energy is depleted, they are ready to take on some additional task and help in any way they can.

Others might receive an "L", denoting *listeners*. These are the people who are always willing to listen to us. They can tolerate our tears and our pain. These are the folks we can call at 3 a.m. knowing they will be honored we reached out to them.

There is one more letter: "R" for *respite*. Grief is hard work. Like any hard work, we need time off from our grief. These are the people who will still share a joke with us or will go to a movie. Often these people confuse us. They never seem to ask about our loss and they may even be uncomfortable if we speak of our grief. Yet, that is their gift. They give us time away from our grief.

Listing and labeling our support helps us in two ways. First, it reminds us of the importance of respite and those who help us receive it. Also, the list may cause us to question if we are using our support system well. Are we asking our listeners to do and our doers to listen? Do we have expectations that cannot be met by the respite people in our lives?

There is one final thing to remember. Even if we have the best support system in the world, it is useless if we do not ask for help or accept assistance when offered.

—KD

Grief and the Internet

The Internet may be a helpful resource for information and support. We need to be careful about the information we share online and be open to other forms of grief support.

Five good things about grieving online:

1. I can share my experiences and feelings with those who may be far away.

2. I can easily find information that can help me.

3. I can remember my loved one and memorialize him or her online.

4. I can talk more openly with people going through the same thing.

5. I can receive support from all over.

Five things to watch out for when grieving online:

1. I might share too much personal information with people I don't know.

2. Information I find might not be true.

3. Support groups might be unsupervised or not very supportive.

4. Comments made by others might be hurtful or offensive.

5. I might be less likely to find help that might be better for me, such as a local support group or private counseling.

—KD

Giving and Receiving

We are all familiar with the words, "It is more blessed to give than to receive." This truism has been the foundation for charity for more than 20 centuries. It reminds us that we need to be generous because our lives have been filled with so many gifts.

Without denying the importance of this time-honored truth, let us turn it end-for-end and examine an additional possibility for its meaning. Many belief systems emphasize both giving and receiving. Is it not possible that there is sizable blessing in receiving?

Judy's friends were frustrated when she seemed to turn away their many efforts to be of help to her after Alan died. They invited her to come for lunch but she always had an excuse. She said she was too tired to go shopping. She insisted that she wasn't ready to come to church on Sundays. She rejected her brother-in-law's offer to help her with insurance claims and other business details.

Why is it so difficult for some people to accept help? There are many possible reasons. Some folks argue that they do not want to be dependent; they want to show that they can stand on their own two feet. For them, being willing to receive help is a sign of weakness. We live in a culture that values self-reliance and independence, and do not want to be seen as needy.

But haven't you found as you grieve for your loved one that you are needy? Mourners often speak of feeling empty, as if a large part of their life has been drained away. Plans for the future are vacant. Things that provided pleasure no longer offer satisfaction. There is little energy to perform the routine activities that filled your days.

Even your sense of being a person is diminished, empty.

It is not difficult to understand how a person feeling that way turns away offers of help. A low sense of self-worth undercuts seeing anything as a gift. Because a gift implies a giver, the person who feels empty cannot imagine that anyone could care enough for him or her to freely give anything.

So they feel that they are a burden. They assume that people are offering to help out of pity or because they feel they have to. On the other hand, the person who feels a deep sense of belonging (whether it be understood as belonging to God, to the universe, to a family circle or a community of friends) has the self-esteem to see many of the good things that come along as gifts, even undeserved gifts.

When you stop to think of it, this is a pattern that goes back to the very beginning of our lives. In our very first years in this world, we are totally dependent on the nourishment and nurture of others. Our lives survive and prosper only as we receive.

Although we gradually learn to balance this receiving with giving and sharing, we never outgrow our need to receive graciously. In normal days we receive food that has been grown by others, we use products that are manufactured by people we will never know, and we benefit from random acts of kindness.

In times of special need, like our grieving, we are helped by being open to the blessings that come through receiving the offers of help from family and friends who care for us.

—PI

Grieving Privately

My father died a few months earlier and as the year continues I think of him more often and I'm sad. My siblings have joined a bereavement support group. It's not that I don't believe in counseling, but I've never considered going before and I'm not about to start now. I'm just not one of those people who likes going to groups. What can I do on my own?

Your question illustrates that there is no one right way to go through grief. The way people cope with their loss is as unique as our fingerprints. What works for one may not necessarily work for other members in the family. A 'one-size fits all' approach to grief is just not feasible or helpful.

Your siblings have found their bereavement support groups helpful and indeed, many people praise their groups. But it sounds as if you would find it more helpful to cope privately. I would suggest the use of bibliotherapy as one way to help yourself. Bilbliotherapy is an expressive arts therapy that uses books, articles, essays, or poetry to help us understand and work through our grief.

It is helpful because we can often identify with others through their expressions in literature and art. Knowing that others have survived similar problems and coped successfully can be quite a relief when one feels that no one could possibly understand what they are going through. I suggest you speak with your hospice bereavement coordinator, or have your siblings do so, and obtain a list of readings that pertain to the death of a parent.

Sometimes bibliotherapy is combined with writing therapy, or journaling, as a way to help us with our grief. Journaling, like bibliography, can be a therapeutic tool which is more private than attending a group. You never have to share what you've written with anyone else; it is totally private. Journaling can also be a successful tool for stress management. To be helpful, one writes in detail any thoughts or experiences they are having. The writer does not need to worry about spelling, grammar, or sentence structure. It is just a free flow of thoughts. One suggestion I offer my clients who are journaling is to always record the date when you've written something. Grief is often a slow process and it is helpful to look back and see where you were three or nine months ago. Another benefit of journaling is that it can be a way to gain valuable information about ourselves and offer us new insights, helping us to gain clarity. Both bibliotherapy and journaling are two examples of how you can help yourself without including others.

—SS

Condolence Letters

When the first condolence letter arrived in the mail two weeks after the death of her husband, Sandra was a little surprised to open it and read its contents. She remembered all too well how inadequate she had felt when it came to writing condolence letters to the family members of people she knew who had died.

Often, she barely knew those family members, or she was only acquainted with the deceased person in a casual or superficial way. Almost always, she tried to avoid or put off writing letters of condolence.

After all, she asked herself, what could she write that might be appropriate when a death had occurred? It was difficult to think of anything to say that went much beyond familiar clichés like, "I'm sorry for your loss."

Even if she could think of something distinctive to say, Sandra couldn't imagine how bereaved survivors would welcome the few lines that she might write on a note or card. How could her feeble words lessen in any way the grief that family members must feel when they have lost someone they loved?

Sandra had even worried that it would be cruel to send a card or letter of condolence to bereaved family members. She told herself that mentioning a subject that was the source of so much pain would only be like rubbing salt into a wound.

Yet Sandra found the first condolence letter she received to be a bright moment in her day. It did make her cry as she thought of her deceased husband, but it also made her feel closer to him.

The letter reminded her she wasn't the only one who had loved her husband. In fact, she could see from this letter and others that followed that he had inspired affectionate feelings and even love from many people who had known him.

Some of the condolence letters told Sandra things about her husband of which she had previously been unaware. Others mentioned some quality in him that the writer had cherished, and often it was a quality that Sandra had also treasured.

Even when people just sent a card to Sandra, she could see that many of them had made an effort to pick out a verse that was appropriate to her situation. Most of them added just a few words to personalize the preprinted text to show that they cared about Sandra and about her husband.

Sandra learned from all of this that sharing with bereaved family members a thought, a sentiment, or a few words about someone who had died is an important act of kindness. It wasn't at all a hurtful or an unnecessary act. Actually, it was a gesture of kindness and solidarity in the face of human mortality and vulnerability.

Sandra resolved that she would encourage all of her friends who had not previously done so to send her a brief card or letter of condolence. She also determined that she would do the same for bereaved family members of someone she had known who had died.

Editor's Note: This article was inspired by a passage in Laurie Graham's book, *Rebuilding the House* (Viking Penguin, 1990).

—*CC*

Moving Forward on the Journey

Keeping the Connection

One of the myths of grief is that we should slowly forget the past and move on with our lives. We are often told that we need "closure." In other words, we need to close this chapter of our life before we begin another.

Nothing can be further from the truth. Grief is not about letting go; grief is about finding ways to continue the connection even as we live a different, now changed life.

Understanding that is important. Sometimes we hold on to the pain of grief believing that if we lose the pain, we will lose the connection. We may believe that the end of grief is the end of memory. In fact, grief is far more complicated. We live, or journey with, our grief. One of the first signs we are doing better is when we can laugh at memories and remembrances that were once too painful to recall.

Even if we wished to, we could not sever the connection. We are tied in too many ways to the person we loved. They still live in our memories, and those memories are evoked as we live our life. For Gina, that is a constant comfort. As she gardens or shops, she remembers her conversations with Paul, the flowers he cherished, and the foods he liked. For me, another event evokes memories years after my father's death. Every time I go to the airport, I get my shoes shined. Before church every Sunday, Dad and I used to go to a shoe-shine stand. It was a very special father-son time, remembered each time I sit for a shine.

The legacies the person has left can be another source of comfort and connection. For Lydia, it is a special grin that her young son

Keith has—one just like his dad's. Every morning, when I write my list of things to do that day, I know that this was a habit taught by my dad.

The people we love are part of us and part of our own biography. Our parents, our siblings, and our spouses have left an indelible mark on who we are. We may have unusual moments when we feel this connection. One young boy told me that while his grandma had died, she was still alive in his dreams. Others may feel someone's presence or have an occurrence where they seem to smell, hear, or even see someone who died. Others may have a more symbolic experience. For Maria, the sight of butterflies is a visible connection to her sister; she seems to see them at moments when she needs or misses her the most. Still others may find the sense of someone they love in the comments of others. All of these experiences, however they occur, reaffirm a sense of connection.

Our spirituality, however we understand it, offers a sense of this connection. To my young granddaughter, her maternal grandmother is now "Grandma in heaven." Others may see the person living on in memory or perhaps in a different form. Yet, each of us finds connection in our own beliefs.

These connections sustain us even as we struggle with living life without the person we love. That is difficult enough. We need not burden ourselves with the thought that we now have to forget what was, and is, so important a connection.

—KD

What Happens to Grief?

What happens to our grief after we've encountered the death of someone we love? Does it just fade away or somehow disappear? Or does it stay with us always?

In my conversations with many bereaved people over the years, there seem to be two basic ways they describe what happened to their grief. Some say that over time their grief receded or dissipated. According to this account, grief becomes less intense as the pain associated with the loss gradually lessens. People who describe the course of their grief in this way frequently mention the idea that "time heals." While some say this feels true, a wise colleague once observed, "It is not the time we have to use, but the use we make of the time we have."

So an alternative way of phrasing the basic question in this article is to ask: What does time contribute to an individual's journey with grief, if anything? A second important way bereaved people have described what happens to their grief following a loss is to say that they have learned to live with it. Here, the view is that the grief remains, but the individual finds ways to accept or accommodate its presence in his or her life.

It used to be suggested that the central process in an individual's bereavement involved withdrawing emotional energy from the person who died, instead of keeping an attachment. To many, this appeared to mean that we should forget and no longer love the person who died. Not surprisingly, most bereaved people have been horrified by this point of view.

More recently, the academic literature has followed comments from bereaved people who say that what they have done is learned to love the deceased person in a different way. That is, even though they have been separated by death, they still love that person, and feel connected to that person, but acknowledge that the relationship is different.

They maintain the bond by changing it. Not everyone wants to or does establish new relationships with living people, but we all know many people who do remarry or form new attachments without giving up their love for a former spouse or partner who has died.

New attachments become possible because those who survive the death of a loved one restructure the relationship with that person. Perhaps that explains what happens to their grief. It remains, but in an altered form, one that is a bit less intense because it is now reacting to a reorganized relationship. They continue to love, but in a different way.

—CC

Anniversary Blues: Normal and Difficult

"**M**y husband died just over a year ago," a widow said when we met in my office. "Everyone reminds me it has been a year. I seemed to be doing so well for a while. Now I'm depressed again." She is not alone in her reaction.

For many people, the anniversary of the death is a down time. We remember each date vividly. *This is the day he went to the hospital. Today she slipped into a coma. The funeral was a year ago.*

A year takes on a magical quality. We believe that if we survive the first year everything will be much better. Then the year goes by and we don't feel all that different. We may become depressed and dispirited; when we do, it's important to realize that these "anniversary reactions" are normal.

Most people take longer than a year to work through grief. The question after the first year is not if we're feeling better, but if we're feeling better more of the time.

Recognize that the anniversary of the death is a difficult time; just accepting this fact may be of some comfort.

Some other tips may also be helpful as you deal with the anniversary of your loved one's death.

Do what helps you. Take off from work to relax, or if it makes you feel better, keep busy and involved. A mass, memorial service, dedication of flowers, or a visit to the cemetery may give focus to your feelings and provide a sense of comfort. A quiet dinner with family and friends may also help.

Decide who you wish to be with. Not only do we need to decide what to do, we may need to decide with whom we would like to be. It may be necessary to spend some time alone; it may be helpful to spend some time with others. Be respectful of others' needs as they, too, approach the anniversary.

Be patient. Don't expect too much from yourself. Over time, each anniversary will become less difficult. Yet recognize that other holidays, anniversaries, and even happy events such as weddings or births, may renew a sense of loss.

Acknowledge that a loss inevitably changes our life. In time we will be able to think of the person who died without the great pain we experience, even after a year. The great ups and downs of the roller coaster of grief will flatten; there may be some small bumps, but the intensity of the experience will be less. When the work of grief seems so hard and slow, we need to recall that promise.

—KD

The Parental Bond Continues

Part of parenting is asking the continual questions—where are the children, and are they okay? For bereaved parents, these questions take on a challenging new meaning. Although death ends a life, it does not end a relationship. Grief was once understood as the process of severing bonds with the dead person and forming new attachments. Today, we believe that continuing bonds can be a healthy part of the survivor's life.

The concept of continuing bonds is not equated with "denial." Bereaved parents know their child is dead. The continuing bond with the child develops within the overwhelming pain the child's death has brought.

One way bereaved parents stay connected with their dead child may be through "linking objects." These are things connected with the child's life that evoke the child's presence. Six years after his son's death, a father wrote a birthday letter:

Your little wind-up toy, the one of Donald Duck sitting in a shoe, sits on top of the file cabinet in my study. I feel close to you when I'm close to your favorite things.

Parents may also use faith traditions or rituals to keep that sense of closeness. One mother described feeling her daughter's presence when her favorite hymn is sung during church. Another mother wrote a letter as if from the child:

I would have been 20 today, bound by earthly constraints. I am forever, I am eternal, I am ageless. Remember me with love and laughter and yes, with pain. For I was, I am, and I will always be. Once Amy, now nameless and free.

Through continuing bonds, the child can become part of the parent's self. The experience of losing a child may give parents a sense of reinvigorated life and renewed meaning. One parent expressed the feeling this way, "I came to the decision that I was to try to use my gift of life to the utmost as my son had used his." Many bereaved parents try to make the world a better place, as a way of continuing their bond with their child.

These ways of maintaining continuing bonds are not exclusive. Bereaved parents can retain the linking objects from early in their grief while at the same time finding the presence of the child within religious rituals. They can remember the child at the same time they incorporate the child into their own sense of selfhood.

With the help of the continuing bond parent's lives can be rich again, though in a different way. In that sense, the children are there and okay.

—DK

Embrace the Life You Had Before

When Dottie's husband died, she felt totally weighed down by all of the losses associated with his death. Dottie and Bud had no children or grandchildren, and their lives had been closely bound together during their lengthy marriage.

For a long time, all Dottie could think about was what she had lost and what she no longer had. What she missed most were the simple things she shared with Bud. She missed how he would call her "Hon" and kiss her on the back of the neck when she was working at the kitchen sink. She missed Bud's presence alongside her in bed at night, even how he kept the bed warm when it was cold outside.

She missed their everyday routines and having someone to talk to during the news reports they watched after they both came home from work. She even missed having someone to blame when little things went wrong around the house or were left undone.

Sometimes Dottie thought there were so many things she missed that she didn't know how she could go on.

It is hard to take up life again after such a powerful loss. One way to help yourself do that is contained in an old slogan: "Embrace the life you had before."

In the immediate aftermath of an important death in our lives, it is difficult to see beyond all that we have lost. But that's never the whole story. We also have the whole of our lives that occurred before this loss.

It may be helpful for Dottie, as it has been for many other bereaved persons, to recall the life she had shared with her husband. In doing so, Dottie and others will agree that the life they had before was rich in many ways—not perfect, but full of many activities, events, and simple times together whose memories and legacies warm their hearts.

Going back even further, Dottie and other widows acknowledged that before they were married, they each had another life that was also good in many ways. Their marriages built upon those earlier lives; they did not destroy them or empty them of all value.

The challenge for the bereaved is to carry forward and build upon the years they enjoyed with their spouse or partner. It is never easy, but it helps to embrace the life that you had before.

Go over your memories of all the good times you shared with the person you loved (and still love). Search through your house for photographs and other objects that can serve as links to help you recall some of those good times that perhaps you haven't thought about for many years.

Talk to old friends and ask them to share their memories of times they spent together with you and the person who died, or perhaps share memories of the moments they were with that person alone. Don't just set aside the life that you had with the person who died as if it had no impact on your present or future.

Embracing the life you had before is one way to begin embracing the life you have now and will have in the future.

—CC

Times to Remember

When my wife and I downsized to move to a retirement community, large boxes of old family photographs were a problem. There were pictures of our childhoods, our graduations, our wedding, and our children. There were also stacks of fading browned portrait photos of great-grandparents, girls in high shoes and large hair ribbons, baby boys in long christening dresses. Some of these people had died long before I was born, others I had known as a child.

It was so difficult to decide what to do with all those pictures. I had a sentimental attachment to many of them, but there was something more than that. I felt a sense of responsibility because I was a custodian of the fading tangible ties to those who were no longer with us. The boxes are now in my den closet. I had to keep them, and I hope my son will keep them when I'm gone.

This experience convinced me of the value, even the necessity, of preserving memories of the past. Dumping these boxes into the trash would have been the loss of the reminders of those of who have been part of my life, through their DNA, through their nurture, in shared times of pleasure, in the pain of separation and loss. I would have shrunk as a person, because my memories are part of who I am.

We keep mementos: watches, jewelry, clothing, furniture. As we use them, we recall our loved one. *This was my Dad's watch; whenever we use the good china, I think about all the great family holiday dinners Mom had.* Every one of these mementos is a link in the chain of memories.

Your faith community offers you some ways to remember. At the funeral service a eulogy might have been given or stories told of the life that had been lived. There may have been a time of remembrance when family and friends could share treasured memories. Many Protestant churches have annual services in which those who have died during the past year are remembered. Roman Catholics participate in memorial masses. Jewish families observe the Yahrzeit marking the anniversary of the death. These are all valuable ritualized paths to remembrance.

Why is memory so important? We know that memory is a critical part of the grieving process. After the death of a loved one, mourners move slowly from experiencing a living relationship to a relationship of memory. One of the major goals of grieving is to hold a memory of the person who has died. This is the way in which we maintain some connection to the one who has died. We are painfully aware that the kinds of relationship we had in life came to an end when our loved one died. However, those who died did not simply disappear into oblivion. They are still part of our lives, but now in the form of memory.

This is not unhealthy or morbid. A generation ago there was an expression used when talking about someone who had died: "_____, of blessed memory." This was recognition that our memories are indeed a blessing.

Although memories may make us feel temporarily lonely, they are also a connection, a form of relatedness. Memories are the way by which we never lose our loved ones.

—PI

New Relationships

When a spouse dies, his or her partner, somewhere down the road, must decide whether or not to begin a new relationship.

It is not an easy choice. While you may wish for the presence of another loving relationship, there may be other feelings or fears as well. There is no right answer, as grief is individual. There are, however, a number of things you should consider if you decide to date again.

Do not rush the decision. Rushing into a new relationship is as unfair to a respective mate as it is to you. Be sure of your own motives. Are you ready for a relationship or merely seeking to fill time?

Do not compare. For better or worse, you cannot replace the relationship you had. Nothing is more corrosive than constantly comparing your new love to your old.

Be aware of your emotions. It is natural to have a lot of feelings as you embark on a new relationship. These may include feelings of guilt and anxiety. Sort them out with a counselor or close friend.

Introduce your new relationship slowly to your family. Remember that even adult children may be resentful and need reassurance and time. While the opinion of children—at any age—ought to be considered, remember that only you can and should decide whether you are ready to date.

Remember that grief is a lifelong journey. Your deceased spouse or partner will always be part of your life.

—KD

Not the Person I Was

The second anniversary of the death of a loved one often inspires a spouse or partner to look back on who she was before the death and who she has become since. Karen engaged in this type of reflection when she told a friend that it had led her to an important conclusion.

"I've decided," she said, "that I'm no longer the person I was before Jack's death."

What Karen meant was that when her husband was alive she had a pretty clear idea of who she was and had become comfortable with the person she had become. During that time, she knew herself as Jack's wife, a mother, a daughter, a sister, and many other things. All of these were roles that life had given her or that she had chosen.

The death of her husband seemed to challenge many of these parts of her identity. Of course, Karen wasn't changed completely. Many of her roles still continued, as a mother and a sister. But so much of what had been important to her seemed like it had been thrown up for grabs.

A death or a major loss in life transforms you. It changes how you see yourself and how you view your identity.

As Karen went on with her reflection, she said, "Maybe I've even been changed for the better in some ways. I think now that I'm more sensitive to the needs of other people and more caring. I know now that I can't 'fix' other people's grief. I can be there for them and listen to their concerns and try to share with them that much of what they are experiencing is normal for everyone who is bereaved.

"So, if I'm not the person I was before Jack's death, I hope I'm a better person—at least in some ways. I think I paid a high price to become this new person. And, to be honest, if I could have Jack back, I'd make that choice in a second and go back to being the person I used to be."

It's only fair to say that not everyone who experiences the death of someone they love or a major loss becomes a better person like this. Some people find themselves stuck in what seems to be an endless cycle of grief and depression. They go round and round about their losses and their sadness. It is as if they seem always to be so alone, unable to lift up their heads and find some way to move forward with their own lives.

In the end, at least part of what goes on in bereavement is what we make of it. That can be so strange and so hard and so difficult when one is right in the middle of it all. All of this can be helped if we have good friends to turn to, especially when they are people who have experienced similar losses. Such people know enough to try to be available, to listen, and, just by being themselves, to provide models and options as a person copes with loss.

—*CC*

Grief is a Journey

One of the most enduring and complex questions I hear when I lecture about grief is one about *hope.* Can there be hope that the pain presently experienced will ease? For many grievers, the fear of the answer being "no" seems to promise a bleak future. Others ask the question for a different reason. They wish recognition of the continuing bond they retain with the person who died, understanding that pangs of pain are the cost of that connection. So some fear that an answer of "yes" invalidates their connection and their grief.

It is more than the desires and expectations of those asking the questions that make it complex. Grief is highly individual. One person's experiences and needs of grief are different than another's. More critically, the answer depends on how grief, and that easing of the pain, is defined. In my own work, I like to avoid terms like *recovery, healing,* or *resolution.* Recovery means you get back what you once lost. If I lose my cell phone and recover it, I now have my phone again. Resolution suggests that everything is now tied up in a sufficient way. To continue the analogy, the resolution is that I now have a new cell phone. Neither definition works for grief. Healing is also not always useful, as it suggests that I now have returned to a prior equilibrium, though I still may carry a scar reminding me of the loss.

Grief is more like a journey. We live with our loss. We carry that loss with us through our life. But there is an answer to that question about what to hope for.

Over time and with work, the pain of our loss does lessen. We can now function similarly to the way we did earlier. Some may even function better—mastering new skills, appreciating emerging strengths, or developing deeper insights as a result of the loss. However, there still may be surges of grief as we continue to remember the person in varied points or certain events of our life.

Certainly the pang of pain that we may experience may very well be part of what we carry as we move along this journey. We need to be mindful that, over time, it is neither helpful nor a useful legacy to the deceased to live in a state of chronic loss. Individuals can find new meaningful lives even in the face of their losses. As one mother put it, "I learned to live again."

Such an understanding of grief gives the essential promise that the intense pain of grief will not be forever. Yet, it does acknowledge that grief is not something we get over—it is a process, a journey, that becomes part of a new, even more meaningful, life.

—KD

Authors

Kenneth J. Doka (Editor), PhD, MDiv, is a professor of gerontology at the Graduate School of The College of New Rochelle and senior consultant to the Hospice Foundation of America. A prolific author and editor, Dr. Doka serves as editor of HFA's *Living with Grief*® book series, its *Journeys* newsletter, and numerous other books and publications. Dr. Doka has served as a panelist on HFA's *Living with Grief*® video programs for 20 years. Dr. Doka was elected president of the Association for Death Education and Counseling (ADEC) in 1993. In 1995, he was elected to the Board of Directors of the International Work Group on Death, Dying, and Bereavement and served as its chair from 1997-99. ADEC presented him with an Award for Outstanding Contributions in the Field of Death Education in 1998. In 2006, Dr. Doka was grandfathered in as a mental health counselor under New York's first state licensure of counselors. Dr. Doka is an ordained Lutheran minister.

Betsy Beard is a mother who, after the death of her only son Army Specialist Bradley Beard in 2004, found help, hope, and healing in the Tragedy Assistance Program for Survivors (TAPS). She has served as the editor of TAPS Magazine since 2008.

Bonnie Carroll is the President and Founder of the Tragedy Assistance Program for Survivors (TAPS), the national Veterans Service Organization providing front line comfort and care for all those grieving the death of a loved one serving in the Armed Forces. Ms. Carroll founded TAPS following the death of her husband, Brigadier General Tom Carroll, in an Army plane crash. A former board member of the Association of Death Education and Counseling, Carroll has spoken and written on traumatic grief in the military over the past two decades. Carroll is a Major in the Air Force Reserve, where she has served as Chief, Casualty Operations. She held Presidential Appointments in the Reagan and Bush Administrations. Ms. Carroll holds a degree in Public Administration from American University and has completed Harvard University John F. Kennedy School of Government's Executive Leadership Program.

Charles A. Corr, PhD, is Vice-Chair, Board of Directors, Suncoast Institute, an affiliate of Suncoast Hospice in Clearwater, FL. Dr. Corr is also a member of the International Work Group on Death, Dying, and Bereavement (Chairperson, 1989-1993), the Association for Death Education and Counseling, the ChiPPS (Children's Project on Palliative/Hospice Services) Communications Work Group of the National Hospice and Palliative Care Organization, and the Executive Committee of the National Donor Family Council. Dr. Corr has written numerous books, articles, and chapters in professional journals, in the field of death, dying, and bereavement. His most recent publications include two chapters in *Beyond Kübler-Ross: New Perspectives on Death, Dying, and Grief* (Hospice Foundation of America, 2011) and the seventh edition of *Death & Dying, Life & Living* (Wadsworth, 2013), co-authored with Donna M. Corr.

Donna M. Corr, RN, MS in nursing, took early retirement from her position as professor in the nursing faculty of St. Louis Community College at Forest Park, St. Louis, MO. Her most recent publication is the seventh edition of *Death & Dying, Life & Living* (Wadsworth, 2013), co-authored with Charles A. Corr. She has authored numerous publications, book chapters, and articles in professional journals.

Earl A. Grollman, DHL, DD, is a rabbi, lecturer, and a pioneer in crisis management. He is the author of more than 27 books on coping with death and bereavement. In recognition of his contributions to the field, he has received awards from numerous organizations, including the Association for Death Education and Counseling, The Compassionate Friends, and the Visiting Nurse Association. He became the first recipient of the Earl A. Grollman Award in Bereavement endowed by Children's Hospice International, and was named as "Hero of the Heartland" for his invaluable assistance in the Oklahoma City bombing.

Paul E. Irion, MDiv, was the founding president of Hospice of Lancaster County. He also served on the faculty of the Lancaster Theology Seminary of the United Church of Christ for over 25 years. Rev. Irion has written numerous books on death and dying and has been recognized by the Association for Death Education and Counseling for his pioneering work in death and bereavement education.

Dennis Klass, PhD, is a retired professor. He began his work in thanatology at the University of Chicago, where he worked with Elisabeth Kübler-Ross. He is on the editorial boards of *Death Studies* and *Omega, The Journal of Death and Dying.* Klass was the professional advisor to the St. Louis chapter of Bereaved Parents for over 20 years. In that role he did a long-term ethnographic study of parental bereavement. For the last two decades Klass focused his research on the cross-cultural study of grief. He is the author of numerous books, articles, and book chapters.

Patricia Loder is the Executive Director of The Compassionate Friends, a national organization that provides highly personal comfort, hope, and support to every family experiencing the death of a son or a daughter, a brother or a sister, or a grandchild, at any age. Mrs. Loder first became involved with The Compassionate Friends after her children Stephanie and Stephen died when their car was struck by a speeding sport motorcyclist. She has written many stories regarding grief and bereavement following the death of a child and is a frequent workshop presenter and grief speaker.

Paul A. Metzler, DMin, an Episcopal priest and psychotherapist, is director of Community Education for the Visiting Nurse Service of New York Hospice and Palliative Care program. He also serves as the spiritual care coordinator for the VNSNY Hospice IPU Specialty Care Unit. Metzler is a Fellow of the American Association of Pastoral Counselors, a NYS licensed marriage and family therapist, and a member of the American Association for Marriage and Family Therapy, the Association for Death Education and Counseling, the Council of Hospice Professionals, Spiritual Directors International, and the Assembly of Episcopal Healthcare Chaplains. He is an associate priest of the Church of the Transfiguration in Manhattan and the Church of the Holy Innocents in West Orange, NJ.

Sherry R. Schachter, PhD, FT, is the director of Bereavement Services for Calvary Hospital/Hospice in New York where she develops, coordinates, and facilitates educational services for staff and develops and oversees an extensive bereavement program for families and bereaved members of the community. Dr. Schachter also directs Camp Compass®, the hospital's summer camp for bereaved children and adolescents. Dr. Schachter is a recipient of the prestigious Lane Adams Award for Excellence in Cancer Nursing from the American Cancer Society and for over 30 years has worked with dying patients and their family caregivers. She is a past president of the Association for Death Education and Counseling and a member of the International Work Group on Death, Dying and Bereavement. Dr. Schachter is an international speaker and is widely published on issues related to dying, death, and loss.

Harold Ivan Smith, PhD, serves on the teaching faculties of Saint Luke's Hospital in Kansas City, MO, and the Carondolet Medical Institute in Eau Claire, WI. He is a member of the Association for Death Education and Counseling. Dr. Smith is the author of numerous publications on grief and bereavement.

Judy Tatelbaum, MSW, LCSW, is a psychotherapist in Carmel, CA, an inspirational speaker, workshop leader, and professional trainer. She authored the books *The Courage to Grieve* and *You Don't Have to Suffer.* She trains people in dealing with catastrophic illness, grief, death and dying. Ms. Tatelbaum has been a long-time contributor to *Journeys.*

Nancy Boyd Webb, DSW, BCD, RPT-S, is a leading authority on play therapy with children who have experienced loss and traumatic bereavement. Dr. Webb was a professor on the faculty of the Fordham University School of Social Service from 1979 until 2008, where she held the endowed James R. Dumpson Chair in Child Welfare Studies, and in 1997 was named University Distinguished Professor of Social Work. In 1985 she founded Fordham's Post-Master's Certificate Program in Child and Adolescent Therapy which continued for 22 years until her retirement.

Sister Marilyn Welch, CCW, is a victims' advocate and the Coordinator of Protecting God's Children.

Mary Grace Whalen, MS, is a freelance writer with over 50 articles published to date on grief, hearing loss, disability, aging and baby boomer issues. Ms. Whalen is an Adjunct Professor at SUNY Westchester Community College where she teaches literature and writing courses.

Elizabeth Uppman is a writer and mother of two living in Overland Park, KS. Her essays have appeared in *Good Housekeeping,* Salon.com, *Brain, Child* Magazine, and other publications. She is currently working on a memoir.

Ellen Zinner, PsyD, earned a doctorate in clinical psychology and was certified as a grief counselor and grief educator by the Association for Death Education and Counseling (ADEC). She joined ADEC in its first year of existence and served as the organization's president in 1991-92, chaired numerous ADEC committees, and co-chaired two national conferences. She also served as president of the Maryland Psychological Association. Dr. Zinner began her academic career in death education teaching university courses and went on to write numerous articles, chapters, and one book in the field.

Journeys

A newsletter to help in bereavement

JOURNEYS: A NEWSLETTER TO HELP IN BEREAVEMENT

Journeys is Hospice Foundation of America's monthly newsletter offering support and practical advice for people coping with loss and grief. Each month, _Journeys_ features articles written by experts in an easy-to-read style that speak to the many different aspects of the grieving process. Regular monthly features include expert answers to reader questions.

JOURNEYS SPECIAL ISSUES

HFA publishes Special Issues of _Journeys_ in a range of topics, helping individuals at particularly difficult times of the year. Don't miss out on some of the best resources available for those struggling with grief and loss.

Journeys special issues include:

- Newly Bereaved Issue
- Anniversary Issue
- For Kids By Kids (Teen)
- Understanding Support Groups
- Winter Holidays
- Spring Holidays
- Caregiving and Hospice
- Child Loss

WORDS FROM OUR READERS

"The newsletters were very, very helpful and reassuring. I looked forward to them and (they) were always what I needed."

"What has helped me a lot are your Journeys _pamphlets; it's a great help for me to read that other people may be going through the exact same grieving as I am. This really helps me."_

"Love the monthly paper Journeys— _very close to the heart happenings."_

_"_Journeys _has been very helpful for our Hospice families and staff. We are grateful to have access to the important and useful information you provide."_

ORDERING INFORMATION

Subscribing to or ordering _Journeys_ is easy. _Journeys_ is available online at **store.hospicefoundation.org** or by phone at **1-800-854-3402**.

If you have any questions, just call—HFA staff will be happy to help you.